HAUNTED GETTYSBURG

EYE
WITNESS ACCOUNTS
OF THE
SUPERNATURAL

by
Jack Bochar
Bob Wasel

**Published and Distributed
by
Americana Souvenirs & Gifts
206 Hanover Street
Gettysburg, PA 17325**

Contents

To Ashley and Stephanie
BW
To my children and grandchildren
JRB

PREFACE

Have you ever had a strange 'feeling' or experienced *Déjà vu* while on the Gettysburg battlefield? Perhaps you thought you saw someone or something that vanished inexplicably before your eyes, or maybe you heard voices and sounds where, plainly no one was visible. Why do so many people report strange occurrences on the battlefield of Gettysburg? It seems the town has far more than its share of supernatural incidents, almost all in some way connected to the battle. Those affected can be men, women, or children, just about anybody who ventures onto the hallowed grounds, ever-soaked with the blood of thousands. Some of these soldiers ended their natural lives suddenly, others lingered painfully until gasping their last breath. Why then, is Gettysburg so abundantly haunted?

With the circumstances surrounding the Battle of Gettysburg, one can see many reasons. Look at some of these conditions. Most of the soldiers were young, no more than mere teenagers. When a man is older, he begins to take on characteristics both physically and mentally to prepare him inevitably for death. As his face takes on wrinkles and his hair grays, he knows he is getting closer to 'the beyond' with his body adjusting through the years. When death does come, he is usually more peaceful and accepting of his fate, but when death comes to a young man, they do not accept it as easily. For a young man, so full of life, death is very unfamiliar, probably the furthest thing from his mind, thinking it can never happen to him. So, for many young men who met a violent death at Gettysburg, the change was too abrupt, never expected. It is thought that their soul is less at rest and not at peace, and therefore, their spirit remains forever where they died, until they can make peace. Another reason spirits are thought to haunt is that when a person dies in unfamiliar surroundings, as did thousands of Union and Confederate soldiers hundreds of miles from home, they roam the fields searching for their homes or friends. One reason they so haunt the battlefield, occurs when a person dies a violent death, such as the scores of men that fell at Gettysburg. It has been said that when a violent death occurs, the spirit of the person goes into a nearby inanimate object, such as a rock or boulder. When one looks at the number of casualties and vast number of rocks on the battlefield, such as the front of Little Round Top and Devil's Den, it is conceivable that each rock could contain the restless spirit of a soul lost to the tragic battle. It is no wonder then, that there is such an abundance of spiritual activity so frequently taking place on old battlefields. This book was written to share a number of peoples' encounters with the bizarre, unexplainable, or supernatural spirits on the battlefield of Gettysburg.

This project required the assistance of many and we are very thankful to all who have contributed. We wish to acknowledge those who provided generous help, Diane Bochar, Nancy Calderwood, Sarah Richardson, and Thomas Winter, jr. Without their help, in the form of editorial assistance, suggestions on the format of the book, stories, etc., this book could not have been written.

INTRODUCTION

Presented here are some stories reported to the authors and it is left entirely up to you to decide whether you are willing to believe in the spirits of Gettysburg or not. Most of these stories have happened recently and for the most part do not include folklore. A considerable number of Civil War reenactors making contact with apparitions have been noted. One explanation would be the uniformed reenactor is possibly a familiar sight to the wandering spirits in search of a companion or friend. Because some contributors of these stories requested not to include their name for fear of ridicule by nonbelievers, the authors thought it best to change all names for anonymity. They do not claim any of the stories to be factual, narrating them as told to them, left to your judgment whether or not one chooses to believe their contents. The stories are meant solely for your entertainment and enjoyment.

As for the authors, the first time they visited Gettysburg, the thought of a ghost or spirit never occurred to them. In fact, the whole idea of haunts was quite unbelievable and only 'weird' people would believe such nonsense. Their first day on the battlefield was overwhelming with the large number of monuments and the plaques containing their accounts of the fight. It was a beautiful fall day in late October and after almost a full day of visiting the battlefield, they returned to the town talking about their tour-filled day. While in town they thought the Jennie Wade House would be interesting. Many strange occurrences have been associated with the Jennie Wade house, Jennie's relationship with Wesley Culp and Jack Skelly, and the tragic end to her young life. It is a fact that many people experience oddities, strange sensations, and many unexplained occurrences upon entering the Jennie Wade House. The authors of this book had their first experience with the strange, if not bizarre, incidents associated with the purported possessed house. As they visited the Jennie Wade House, they gathered for a tour, a very small tour, only the two of them and one woman. While waiting for the tour to begin, conversation started among all, and the woman could think of nothing else to talk about but the house. She told them that she had just arrived in Gettysburg for the first time. Accompanied by her husband, she stopped in a local shop to pick up a brochure describing the Jennie Wade House. She said the brochure contained not only a brief description of the house, but also included a photograph of Jennie Wade. She looked at the photo of Jennie and was startled — it bore an uncanny resemblance to her daughter. She told them it saddened her after seeing the picture because her daughter had died and, looking at the photo, reminded her of her own painful disaster. After seeing the brochure, she told them she felt compelled to go to the Jennie Wade house, not knowing why, just knowing she felt beckoned. Even stranger, the woman's daughter's name was — Jennie. After showing her husband the brochure, the photo of Jennie Wade so disturbed him, that he could not bring himself to go to the Wade House. As the woman nervously toured the house, she told them another unnerving fact. Her daughter Jennie tragically died at the age of twenty during July — just as did Jennie Wade.

The authors decided to revisit the battlefield after departing the Jennie Wade House, so they got into the car and headed down Emmitsburg Road to the park entrance of the battlefield. By then, 8:00 P.M., it was quite dark and the battlefield was empty of any tourists — except them.

The night was without fog, and the sky was black as pitch as they slowly drove through the winding tree-lined roads. The air had a slight chill, but not enough to prevent the opening of their windows as they continued. As they turned a corner and the road straightened out, the appearance of seven young men suddenly startled them. The men, dressed in some type of uniforms and lined up at attention side-by-side at the edge of the road, all saluted them as they slowly drove by in wonderment. After they passed by them, with their mouths opened, they looked at each other puzzled by what they had just seen. They turned the car around for another look, but to their astonishment — the 'soldiers' were no longer there — they'd vanished! They questioned what they just witnessed and coming to no sensible conclusion, left the incident alone.

They continued through the wooded area, still not encountering a single car in the dark and stillness of the night. Through the open windows they thought they heard a muffled shot and stopped the car, turning off the engine. Sure enough, they heard more of what sounded like muskets firing in the distance, then an occasional cannon shot. This went on for about thirty seconds and the quietness again took over. After hearing the shots they thought a reenactment of some sort was taking place on the battlefield, dismissing the notion of anything out of the ordinary occurring.

They drove about another hundred yards when, for some

unknown reason, they decided to stop again, this time leaving the confines of the car. They walked a short distance along the road, talking about the battlefield, when one of them suddenly stopped and said, "Shh — what's that? Who is walking behind us? Do you hear the footsteps?" Listening very intently, the other heard nothing, but both of them felt a strange sensation that someone was there and they quickly made their way to the safety of the car.

By now they were somewhat nervous but neither would admit to the other the fear starting to take over, after all, they were adult men. Starting the engine, too proud to confess their apprehension, they again continued their journey making their way to General Lee's monument, parking the car and walking to the statue. As they talked, they held a lighter up to look at a monument. As Jack continued reading, he did not notice Bob rush to the car. Bob, who was then sitting in the car, suddenly interrupted exclaiming in a terrified voice, "Are you coming? Are you coming? Didn't you hear it?" Not hearing a single noise, Jack joined startled Bob in the car to find out what the excitement was all about. He said, "Didn't you hear that? The loud crashes through the woods right next to us? It was so loud, how could anyone not hear it?"

Bewildered by the series of strange occurrences that happened to both of them, still not believing anything supernatural could possibly happen, they gathered up enough courage to carry on. What better place to visit at night, they thought, then Devil's Den. Still, the whole time not encountering a single other car, they slowly drove into the parking lot in front of the large boulder's, on that dark, dark night, and parked shutting off the engine — but this time rolling up the windows. They were there not more than a few minutes trying logically to explain everything that happened to them that evening, when a noise outside the car startled them. They both jerked their heads in the direction of the sounds, their hearts began to speed up and pound. As they looked in fright, a hideous-looking goat had its face pressed up against the window, saliva dripping out of its mouth, staring intently at them. Still shaking by the fright, Jack quickly picked up the camera on the front seat, turned on the flash, and snapped the shutter, after which the goat was gone. They said nothing else, not a word, both of them immediately left the battlefield never looking back that night.

The next day they stopped at the visitor's center, asking park rangers about the reenactment the evening before, to which the answer was unanimously, "There was no reenactment and besides, they do not allow firing of weapons on the battlefield." Anxious to see the photograph of the goat at Devil's Den, they had the film processed. To their astonishment, every picture was perfect — except the one of the goat — it was entirely black, no reflection from the flash, no object, nothing! Ever since that event-filled day, they both have a new outlook on the strange and unexplainable occurrences surrounding the Battle of Gettysburg. They will not swear ghosts or apparitions exist, but, on the other hand, absolutely will NOT swear they do not.

Devil's Den

A THIRST FOR THE UNKNOWN

As the sun rose and burned off the lingering fog, another day in Gettysburg began. Among a group of tourists were a young man and woman, Mark and Linda, dressed in Civil War clothes. They got an early start and visited many battlefield sites, like Little Round Top, Devil's Den, and the Wheatfield, on that hot summers day. Absolutely enchanted by the monuments and places of century-old carnage, they could not bring themselves to leave. They stopped only briefly for quick snacks and cold drinks to help alleviate the punishing heat furnished by the unforgiving sun. Soon, Mark and Linda found the day was almost consumed, as it was already late in the evening with very little sunlight remaining. Still thirsty from the day's relentless heat, Mark took a drink from the bottle of soft drink he purchased earlier, but found it to be warm and undrinkable, so he told Linda they should go back to town.

Driving through the battlefield, however, they were impelled to make just another stop before leaving — the High Water Mark. So drawn to, and impressed by that spellbinding area, Mark wanted a keepsake of the moment. Therefore, he directed Linda to sit and pose upon a caisson while he took a photograph. As he focused his camera to take the picture, he noticed a very dark unrecognizable image of some sort behind Linda. Thinking a person's shadow or reflective glare caused the image, Mark slightly moved the camera and began to refocus. To his utter astonishment, the image now took the shape of a man mounted on a horse. As Mark watched through his lens during that instant of time, the man dismounted and the image just as quickly disappeared. Mark still shaken by the incident tried to finish taking the picture but found the camera inoperable. Having another camera in his car, Mark quickly retrieved it, hoping to get another glimpse of the phantom horseback rider. This time, as he looked through the lens and snapped the shutter, he could see Linda as before, however, no other figure appeared in the scene.

As they talked about what had just happened with disbelief, Mark, now thirstier than before, needed to quench his thirst. For some

1

strange unexplained reason he felt compelled to stop yet again at the nearby Cushing monument. Linda was leading the way as she stepped on something in her path, then Mark following, stepped on the same object stopping briefly to kick it out of the way. After viewing the Cushing

Left: Cushing monument *right:* caisson Linda posed by

monument, they returned the way they came, using the same route, and again stepped on the same object Mark kicked aside minutes earlier. Thinking it was a tin can, Mark this time wanted to pick the object up and dispose of it when, to his amazement, saw it was a rusted Civil War canteen.

Mark and Linda are convinced, to this day, that the apparitions of the man dismounting the horse, and the Civil War canteen mysteriously appearing in their path, were supernatural. They believe a spirit from the Battle of Gettysburg attempted to come to the aid of Mark, seeing him as perhaps, a thirsty soldier, on that blistering hot summer day, over one-hundred and thirty years later.

2

MUSIC IN A BOY'S EYE

It all began one hot summer day when Jack took his 2-year-old son, Charles, on a bike ride near their Illinois home. Along the path was a public park, nothing out of the ordinary, old established trees and large green open areas for walking and picnics. A somewhat unusual, large singular boulder stood glistening between two old Oak trees, and accompanied by a nearby plaque. Little Charles for some unknown reason was captivated by that boulder and wanted to go to it and sit upon it. Because Charles insisted, it soon became a regular stop on the bike rides. Charles loved that enchanting boulder, which stood about 4 feet high. It was flat enough on the surface allowing him to sit atop it and play with the toy cars he brought with him.

Camp Kane — Morgan trained here and Charles 'discovered' the Civil War here. Courtesy of St. Charles Heritage Center, St. Charles, IL

After a number of times at the boulder, Jack finally read the plaque and discovered the site was an old Civil War training camp for the 8th Illinois Cavalry, named Camp Kane. The plaque described some of the battles and engagements the 8th fought in, one of which was Gettysburg. Not knowing much about the Civil War, Jack found the plaque interesting and read it to Charles. A spark twinkled in Charles's eyes as he listened with uncommon interest and immediately started

3

playing soldiers, picking up a stick to use as a gun and making the noises of shots - "pow - pow."

As time went on, the compelling stops continued, but Charles was no longer content with just stopping and playing with his small cars and sticks. Now, he brought makeshift clothes simulating uniforms and brought a toy Civil War musket that he made out of wood. His Civil War fever continued to grow and the alluring visits to Camp Kane never ceased.

By the time Charles was nine years old he begged his father to consider being a Civil War reenactor. Reluctant at first, Jack finally succumbed and they began a reenacting outfit called, at the request of Charles - the Eighth Illinois Cavalry. By now Charles actually felt he was a part of the 8th Illinois and told his father, "Dad, you know, I've been at Gettysburg before, in the battle there. I have seen the fighting all around me." Jack hearing this did not think much of it, although Charles had never been east of Illinois in his life. Nevertheless, why would Charles say such a thing? Childhood imagination? Perhaps, but he repeated the statement a number of times and insisted he had been there.

Now that Charles was a member of the 8th Illinois Cavalry as a reenactor, he asked what he had to do to become a bugler. Charles never expressed an interest in playing an instrument before. He never played a musical instrument, nor had a single lesson, in fact, he did not know the difference between a whole note and a half note, nor any other musical terms, but somehow he knew that he could become a bugler. Jack picked up a used bugle, gave it to Charles, and in a matter of a couple weeks he was able to play out a number of Civil War bugle calls. Playing the bugle came to Charles naturally and the little boy played from his soul as if he had previously known the songs. In fact, after Charles heard a bugle call played, he could repeat it without the use of sheet music, playing from within himself. Jack could now see a strange combination of coincidences occurring with Charles — the unexplained allurement to the boulder in Camp Kane at two years old, the overwhelming desire to be a member of the 8th Illinois Cavalry, and now the unexplained yearning and admirable performance as a 11-year-old bugler in the 8th Illinois Cavalry. Still, Jack did not give too much thought to it, after all, lots of children pick up particular skills at a young age and are musically talented; however, in Charles's case it was more than an interest, it was almost an obsession pulling at him.

4

As a reenactor, Charles wanted to take on a name from the original roster of the 8th Cavalry and was reading the roster, when, he suddenly stopped and said "I want this one! That's me!", picking the name Morgan. Not only did he pick out a fascinating name, but as later investigation showed, Charles unintentionally selected a bugler. Jack helped Charles research trooper Morgan and established he was one of the first to sound *Boots and Saddles* at the Battle of Gettysburg, and, he also had the prestigious honor of playing taps at President Lincoln's funeral. Days later, Jack stopped in a museum in the town where Camp Kane was located looking for genealogical research material. While in the museum and accompanied by Charles, Jack was doing his research when Charles told him, "Look, there's a picture of Morgan!". It astonished Jack to see an old photo of a Civil War soldier placed in a display case and labeled "Morgan." Even more astonishing was that he bears an uncanny resemblance to Charles. They looked alike not only in the facial makeup, but their hands also bore a likeness.

Jack inquired about the photo and was told it was just brought in the previous day by Morgan's granddaughter. Obtaining her name, Jack telephoned the granddaughter explaining who he was and his interest in getting a copy of the photo for Charles. She was delighted and invited Jack and Charles to come to her home, which they did without haste. Once there, after seeing Charles, the granddaughter also commented on the uncanny resemblance between him and her grandfather. She had amusing stories to tell about Morgan and mentioned where they buried him, then proceeded to bring out a few personal articles of his, including the bugle Morgan personally used during the Civil War. She told them a few years ago for a Memorial Day outing, it was requested that Morgan's bugle be used to play Taps at a ceremony and would be performed by a member of the military, a well-trained bugle player. As it turned out, she told them, the man picked up the bugle and was unable to get much more than a grunt out of the old battle horn. Apologizing, he told her because of it's age, it was just not possible to use it and instead used a modern bugle. Staring at Morgan's bugle, Charles was beguiled and finally asked if he may be allowed to hold it. "Of course" he was told, and Charles picked up the bugle to examine it. As he touched the bugle, Charles felt a strange excitement, almost a tingling sensation going through his hands. An excited Charles then asked if he may be allowed to try and play it because, as he put it, "Morgan played that actual bugle at Gettysburg and I have to experience it". She reminded him of the previous person who couldn't get any sounds out of it and told Charles he was welcome to try. Charles brought it to his lips and to everyone's amazement, began to play bugle calls. It was the first time the granddaughter heard any sound from that silver-colored bugle. So amazed was the granddaughter, she quickly picked up the phone to call her son so he too could hear the sounds emitted from their ancestor's bugle, by the young 11-year old boy.

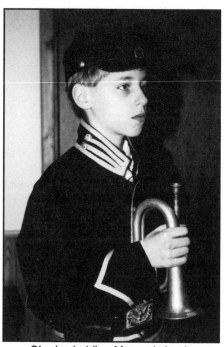

Charles holding Morgan's bugle

Charles insisted on visiting the cemetery Morgan was buried in. Jack agreed to search out the cemetery, knowing only the name of the town and cemetery from the short conversation with Morgan's granddaughter weeks before. Jack drove to the town, found the cemetery, and once there, he was overwhelmed by the large size of the cemetery and wondered how they could possibly find Morgan's grave amongst so many. In a matter of less than 5 minutes Charles walked right up to Morgan's gravestone exclaiming "Here he is!". It was like he was led right to it, just as if he knew right where it was. Charles purposely brought along his bugle with the intention of playing Taps over Morgan's grave, and proceeded to play with a melody eerily echoing throughout the cemetery bringing a tear to his eye. Reading the stone, Jack was amazed when he saw Morgan's birth date — it was that very day! Just another strange coincidence?

The next year Jack and Charles wanted desperately to attend a Civil War reenactment at Gettysburg on July 1st, so they arranged the details and soon arrived in the town. The absolute first place Charles wanted to go was the location of the first day's battle where the 8th Illinois Cavalry, including Morgan, fought. They traveled down the Chambersburg Pike just out of town and stopped at Herr's Ridge. Getting out of the car and walking around, Charles suddenly told Jack, "This is it, this is the place, I know I was here." As it turned out, the 8th Illinois fought on that field and the Herr Ridge Tavern, situated on the ridge, was their headquarters on the morning of July 1, 1863. On that morning in 1863, as they relayed word of the approaching Confederates from the advanced pickets to the officers at Herr's Tavern, buglers at once trumpeted the alert. Morgan was one of the 8th Illinois buglers that day and most assuredly at Herr's Tavern at "the ready", standing by the side of an officer. Can we say for sure that Charles has had a long series of coincidences starting at two years old, all somehow relating to Morgan? Or perhaps, is Morgan somehow reliving through Charles? Charles is now thirteen but still thinks about Morgan frequently. In fact, he has Morgan's photograph on his dresser and every night looks at the picture to bid him a goodnight.

DEADLY DREAMS

When young Johnny was a child, as with any other person, he would dream at night. For Johnny though, he began experiencing not-so-ordinary dreams. Time after time in a reoccurring dream, Johnny would find himself deep within a raging battle. He dreamed of artillery shells fiercely flying in all directions, yells of commands, men shouting and cursing, and carnage everywhere. He then found himself on a large boulder-covered hill and, after more fighting, they compelled him soon to leave his boulder-protected domain. Facing the intense barrage of deadly fire coming his way, he made a heroic charge down the rocky slope of the hill. Running down the hill shouting and, simultaneously, listening to the ever-increasing number of bullets whiz by his body, he took his last step — as a well-directed bullet found its victim — killing Johnny.

When Johnny had these disturbing recurring dreams, he never really knew where the battle was taking place or for that matter, in what war he was unwillingly placed. What he did know though, was that the scenario was repeatedly identical, and the outcome was always the same. The years went on and Johnny was no longer a child yet the puzzling dreams remained with him, very much a part of his life.

On one very eventful day the puzzle would begin to take shape as fate had Johnny traveling through the area and by chance happened to stop in Gettysburg. It was just an ordinary day — or so he thought. With nothing special planned, and some free time on his hands, Johnny decided to tour the Gettysburg battlefield. After stopping in the Visitor's Center and obtaining a battlefield map, Johnny, just as millions of other tourists do, began looking at the monuments and reading their inscriptions. Impressed with the vast number of monuments and immense size of the battlefield, Johnny slowly made his way through the winding roads frequently stopping to read more of the monument inscriptions. The next stop would be the one Johnny will remember for the rest of his life and finally solve his mysterious puzzle.

As he pulled into the parking area atop Little Round Top, he looked around at the dense number of trees. As he looked, he envisioning the battle, then followed the short trail leading to the summit of the hill overlooking the beautiful countryside. In the distance was the Wheatfield, Peach Orchard, and at the bottom of the hill the Valley of Death and the boulders of Devil's Den. Taken in by the beauty and serenity of the scene, Johnny felt a strange sensation urging him to walk down the front slope of Little Round Top.

Slope in front of Little Round Top

Gazing up for one last look at the stoic monument of Gouverneur K. Warren, Johnny began his descent, carefully stepping on, over, and across the many rocks and boulders embedded in the slope of the hill. Suddenly, after walking down part of the hill, Johnny froze in his footsteps as if running into a brick wall. An instantaneous sweat broke out, while his heart began speeding up, and at that very instant in time Johnny knew why all his life the same recurring dream haunted him. Unable to contain himself, he blurted out "Here it is! This is where I was killed!"

Although he does not know what his name was during that battle, Johnny firmly believes, that they killed him there, in that very spot on the slope of Little Round Top. His dreams have no longer puzzled him. Because of his experience at Little Round Top, Johnny now feels a tremendous relief and bizarre sense of peace. Johnny's one and only wish when he departs this world is his desire to be cremated and his ashes placed on that very spot where he died — over one-hundred and thirty years ago.

UNIMAGINABLE HORROR

Two tourists walking down Sickles Avenue were approaching the point where it intersects with Wheatfield Road when they noticed what seemed to be a cloud covering a small field at the intersection. They

Area by Sickles Avenue where dead and dying soldiers were thought to have been attacked by hungry pigs

thought it very strange that the battlefield was not foggy that day, except covering that one section. As they got closer, they thought they heard sounds of men talking along with sounds of distress. They stopped to look for anyone in the area, but without luck. The two were not the only ones to hear voices and sounds coming from that field, as they found out when they asked about the area. This small field unmarked by monuments lacks the majesty of Little Roundtop, the drama of Culp's Hill, and the power of Devil's Den — just a quiet corner of the battlefield. One would hardly notice it, yet this spot witnessed one of the most terrifying scenes

11

of the battle. This little field was host to wounded Union soldiers on the nights of July 2 and 3, 1863, who had fought desperately to hold a salient that reached out from Devil's Den through the Wheatfield to the Peach Orchard and back to Cemetery Hill.   As darkness fell, they found themselves cut off from their fellow troops behind enemy lines. Lying on this field racked with pain and thirst, their life's blood seeping out, they knew the possibility of help from their own troops was slim and, as night descended, they could hear the sounds of troops in the distance and the far off moans and cries of other wounded soldiers.   Still, a new and unimaginable horror would soon unfold that night. Presently, they heard the sounds of soldiers coming through the woods. Could it be help? Was it their own men and safety, or Confederate troops and the possibility of prison camp? At least they might now live. But, what they saw now was a new terror — huge hogs let loose by the destruction of fences of the surrounding farms — and they all knew what that meant. They knew that hogs were known to eat the dead and, worse, the wounded after a battle. That night of July 2 and 3, 1863, as the hungry hogs circled looking for their own spoils of war, these desperately weakened men were forced to hold them off the best they could with bayonets and sabers. Some people believe the distressful sounds of pain and agony can still be heard on that small field, as witnessed by the two tourists.

REENACTING THE PAST

Gettysburg draws many Civil War reenactors to the town and surrounding battlefield, but why? Perhaps because it was the site of one of the most famous battles in American history, or, could it be the close connection between reenactors and the spirit world? We may never know, but what we do know is that an uneven proportion of reenactors have strange encounters and sightings with their counterparts of the past. Several of these stories recently reported follow.

Whispers

A couple of uniformed Civil War reenactors were taking in the sights on the battlefield when they decided to visit Big Roundtop. They were driving at a low speed, with the windows rolled down to allow the best view of the area, making an occasional stop. They crossed Emmitsburg Road and went on at the low speed still taking in the sights, when they heard soft voices in conversation. At first they thought it was the radio but soon discovered it was off. They had a strange desire to find where the voices were coming from and, consequently, believing the sounds to be from a nearby picnic area, drove into it.

Once in the picnic area they found nothing — not a soul to be found. The two men, confused and questioning their own minds, continued their journey to Big Roundtop. Reports of people hearing voices, cannon shots, muskets, and noises of all description, only to find there is no source for the unexplained sounds, are a common occurrence on the battlefield. The next time you hear an unexplained sound while on the battlefield with no visible origin, you might ask yourself, "Do I just hear extraneous noise, or could I be listening to a supernatural experience?"

****

Bangs

Two reenactors dressed in their Civil War apparel, ventured into the Triangular Field wanting to get a first-hand look at the locality. As they passed through the gate and started down a slope of the field, they talked and looked around at the view. Nobody else was in the area, or at least, they saw nobody. All the two men could hear was the muffled noise

Triangular Field

of distant traffic. Soon they were half way down the slope into the field and could no longer hear the traffic. Now what they heard was the distinct firing of cannons and the beating of drums. A quick look around for the origin of the sounds showed nothing but the emptiness of the Triangular Field, void of any other human beings. The two men both agreed that what they had just experienced was an unearthly visit from the past. Not knowing why it had occurred, the reenactors, as they vacated the field, left a token cigarette on a rock inside the gate for the unseen apparitions.

****

Strange Looks
In the evening, around 8:30 P.M., two reenactors, fully dressed in their sharpshooter uniforms, ventured up the hill to the top of Little Round Top. Because of the time of the year, darkness had already set in and the two men were equipped with only a lantern to guide their way. Looking around some, they made their way to the top of the 44th New York Monument to extend their somewhat limited view. One man at first looked to his left, then forward, and finally to his right in the direction of Gouverneur Warren's vigilant statue. Gouverneur K. Warren was the Union officer who, during the Battle of Gettysburg, went atop Little Round Top because it offered a good view of the area to observe enemy actions. While up on the ridge, Warren spotted the Confederates and then

14

was searching for his Union soldiers. The men walked toward the Warren statue, stopping near the boulder with the Signal Corps Memorial Tablet. As one of the reenactors looked at Warren's statue, he was frozen with fright when, to his astonishment, Warren's head shifted twice, looking toward the stunned man. Thinking he was "seeing things," he quickly told his friend to look at the Warren statue and again, the head shifted, looking toward the dazed reenactors. After the two men witnessed the same occurrence, they immediately left, walking briskly away, almost running down the path from Little Roundtop. Remember, the two men were outfitted in Union uniforms — is the spirit of Gouverneur Warren still looking for his Union soldiers?

Statue of Gouverneur K. Warren

FICKLE FINGER OF FATE

Since the Battle of Gettysburg and even before, myriads of tales, sightings and unconventional occurrences associated with Gettysburg have been abundant. One legend, in particular, is worthy of repeating here, for tangible testimony exists to the core of the account.

Near Devil's Den, to the right of Smith's 4th New York Battery, stands a rock, upon which will be found the name, "P. NOEL" carved into it. Some locals in Gettysburg contend that the name P. Noel was simply a battlefield maintenance worker who, many years ago, carved his own name in the rock for reasons only known to him. Others, however, strongly argue that a young girl, named Pauline Noel, was the owner of the name carved in the rock. They said that years ago, Pauline lived in the area on her father's farm. One of life's enjoyments to Pauline was to accompany her father whenever he worked the fields. On one disastrous day, Pauline went with her father as usual, enjoying the farming and his company when, the wagon hit a rock, throwing the young girl off. Horrified and in shock, the father jumped off only to find he was too late. What he witnessed was the lifeless body of his sweet daughter Pauline, mangled — and decapitated.

P.NOEL carved into a rock near Devil's Den

They claim that many people through the years have seen the headless spirit of Pauline Noel roaming the battlefield in search of her head. Legend also maintains that Pauline's spirit, while roaming the battlefield, came upon that rock and, using her fingers, burned her name into that very stone. You may believe whatever you want, but remember Pauline's story when you visit and touch the carved rock. However, — beware to those that dare run their fingers in the etched grooves of P. Noel — there awaits another part of the legend!

17

THE DEVIL MADE HIM DO IT

One of the famous spots on the battlefield, if not the most famous, is, of course, Devil's Den. What makes it so talked about and visited? No doubt, one reason is the beautiful formation of the boulders, but perhaps another reason is the abundance of stories stemming from supernatural experiences in Devil's Den. One such story took place recently on a gorgeous fall day in the month of October.

Two people, George and Millie, avid visitors to Gettysburg, made one of their several yearly trips to the battlefield, bringing along their pet dog on the short trip of one hour. Randomly driving the battlefield, they made their way to the parking lot in front of Devil's Den, exited their car and went along accompanied by their leashed dog.

Although George and Millie frequented Gettysburg, on that day as they approached the facade of Devil's Den, they made a first-time discovery. Found to the right of a large boulder that was cut to allow the road to go through, they found a small cave. Because it was dusk and still having plenty of light left, they decided to explore the contents of the cave. George went back to his car and retrieved his flashlight, then with Millie and the dog, peered inside. Because of the limited and cramped space, they could go no further. Looking deeper inside, they could see it took a bend to their left, then George shined the flashlight in that area. As they looked in that direction, they noticed a most peculiar mist or fog coming from the bend just ahead. Gazing upon the strange fog, they became startled as it slowly moved around the bend, coming in their direction. At once they instinctively started backing up with an urge to run, but were spellbound by what their eyes were experiencing.

The fog now not only approached them, but to their astonishment, began to take the form of a human. As the ghostly figure appeared to them, they both had an overwhelming feeling of a tremendous power or energy emanating from the shape. There was no doubt in their minds, as the phantom looked at them, that they were unwanted and should leave. Remaining in that shape for only a short time, the unexplainable figure dissipated and soon vanished, leaving George and Millie stunned by what had just taken place.

During the sighting of the human-like apparition, in the excitement, George dropped the dog's leash. The dog, standing about five feet in front of the couple, was still looking in the direction of the cave, however, he stood as still as a rock statue. George called for the dog to come but got no response, the dog still not moving at

Entrance to the small cave at Devil's Den

all. The dog appeared to George like a stuffed lifeless toy and he called again but the dog still did not move.

Frightened by all that happened, they wanted to get out of the area as fast as possible. George then ran up and grabbed the leash giving the dog a tug. As he tugged, George watched as the dog, instead of coming, fell over, just as if it were hit over the head with a hammer. Once it hit the ground it "came to life" and began violently to struggle to get up with painful yelps until, after a few moments, could rise. The dog dashed at full speed away from the cave, crying and yelping the whole time. George could barely hold onto the leash, experiencing unknown strength in the dog's pull.

They all ran to the car as the dog furiously scratched on the door trying desperately to get inside. Then, as quickly as possible, they left Gettysburg, shaken and perplexed by what had just happened to them.

Several months later, George and Millie mustered up enough courage and strength to bring themselves to revisit Gettysburg, in particular, Devil's Den. As they approached Devil's Den the dog started whining and became very excited, refusing to leave the safety of the car. After seeing the actions of their dog, George and Millie, reminded of the dreadful experience they encountered at the cave, decided not to stop at Devil's Den. After all, some things are better left unknown. Could it be that during the battle a soldier had used the cave as a safe-haven during the fierce bombardment to avoid the bursting shot and shell, only to die within its walls? Or, perhaps a Confederate soldier was killed trying to protect the Den from the Union attackers and his spirit still roams the rock to ward off unwanted intruders?

-8-

DEATH'S FINAL BLOW

A typical day in Gettysburg began, just like thousands before, with each person going about their business and their own agenda. However, what started as another usual day for a reenactor of the 9th Virginia Cavalry soon became etched in his mind forever. For on that day as he traveled westward on the Chambersburg Pike, in his mind he would experience something nearly as unexplainable as creation itself. These are his words as he described what happened to him on McPherson's Ridge:

It was a beautiful sunny day and I was going to visit a very good friend of mine in Martinsburg, West Virginia, when, as I traveled Chambersburg Pike (Rt. 30) in the vicinity of McPherson's Ridge, it was as if a window in time opened up!

McPherson's Ridge along Chambersburg Pike

I was at this point able to see the men forming up and could hear the shouts of commands from the officers. Then as quickly as it appeared, it disappeared. But then a second time my 'window' was again opened

23

and I was a witness to the true carnage of battle. The sound of musketry was at the same time glorious as well as the sound of an angry beast let loose on earth from Perdition's flames. The cries of the men as they were struck were dreadful, yet, the great grey line was still there. And that smell of spent powder and flames, as if someone opened a vent directly to hell! All this happening in an instant, did once again disappear. However, my story does not end here.

One final time did my 'window' open, and again I was witness to the aftermath of that fateful day. The smell of sulphur and death all about me, the sound of men horribly wounded yet still breathing begging to be taken from this world. The almost supernatural stillness about it all was quite unnerving!

It is my belief to this very day that had I left my car I just might have disappeared from this age to live out my days, no matter how few, in July 1st, 1863, and forward. I cannot deny that there was a moment where I reached for the door handle. I guess it just wasn't right to do at that moment, and so I am able to convey to you my experience by McPherson's Ridge. It is only just to say that, like many others, I was drawn to this small town with the name of Gettysburg.

9

"GO BACK"

One of the favorite actions a Civil War reenactor does while in Gettysburg, is to walk the field of Pickett's Charge. They walk it to honor those who fought there, to get a 'feeling' of what it was like, while trying to imagine the bloodshed during each step of the way. For one Confederate reenactor, it would be an event he will never forget and perchance got more of a 'feeling' than expected.

Rising early one July morning, Bill dressed in his Confederate clothing to walk Pickett's Charge just as thousands before him. It was 6:00 A.M. and he was alone that peaceful warm morning — just him and the large open field of Pickett's advance. He began the trek occasionally pausing to reflect and contemplate about the battle, slowly making his way across

Spot near the High Water Mark where Bill felt something grasping his leg

the field. As he got nearer to the High Water Mark, Bill began to get images in his mind of the slaughter that took place many years ago. After each step he wondered if some poor soul lost his life on the very spot he placed his foot. What pain and agony these young men were going through as they lay there, dying in mass numbers, can only be imagined, as Bill tediously continued onward. Bill finally made his way to the High Water Mark, experiencing an assortment of feelings — sorrow, anger, tranquility. Abruptly, he felt something grasping at his leg, while hearing a voice say "Go back." Startled, Bill instinctively swung around to see who the person was, but to his astonishment, found he was still alone. He wondered if his mind was playing tricks on him or just a wild imagination. Nevertheless, the grabbing of his leg was too forceful and the voices too clear to be envisioned — it must have been real. Bill left the battlefield with the unanswered question of what had just taken place. Could it be, Bill, dressed in a Confederate uniform, was approached by an apparition of a Confederate soldier desperately trying to hold him back from the hopeless charge?

10

WATCH YOUR BACK

On one especially pleasant day, Rebecca, who lives near Gettysburg and frequents the battlefield, while traveling alone, decided to visit the Devil's Den area. As she drove onto the battlefield in the early morning, Rebecca looked at the serene scene surrounding her. She thought to herself, how could such a peaceful place have been such a violent and tragic field of suffering and death. After she parked in the visitor's parking area in front of Devil's Den, Rebecca just sat a few minutes, again thinking about the terrible battle that took place there. She tried to envision Confederate General Longstreet's soldiers as they valiantly charged into the sizable force of General Sickles. First at the Peach Orchard, then, after a vicious fight, continued their onslaught through the Wheatfield making their way to Plum Run, where she now stood.

When Rebecca exited her car, she walked some, at times stopping to enjoy the scenery, but the whole time thinking about the battle. As Rebecca slowly walked up to, then on the small footbridge crossing Plum Run, she stopped and again continued thinking about the terrible battle that took place on that very site. She envisioned the whole area of Plum Run littered with the bodies of soldiers, North and South, already dead or dying an agonizing death. She imagined the blackened sky full of flying lead and exploding shells, accompanied by sounds of screams and moans. She then remembered why they so aptly nicknamed Plum Run *Bloody Run* — because the water flowed red with the vast amount of blood from the wounded and dead.

As Rebecca stood there pondering about the bloodshed, she began to get strange feelings, no longer did she just think about the battle, she now detected a sensation of someone around her. She knew when she walked up to the bridge, she had not seen a single other person, but she looked around and again, found herself alone. All of a sudden, she sensed a sort of chill, still feeling she was not alone, and not understanding what was occurring, decided it was definitely time to leave.

Moments later, as Rebecca stood on the footbridge, she suddenly felt hands forcefully grabbing her from behind and in an instant was violently thrown off the bridge, landing hard, receiving scratches and bruises. As the dazed woman regained her senses, she impulsively looked all around for the perpetrator, but to her absolute shock, there was no one

Footbridge from which Rebecca was thrown off

to be found. Rebecca quickly picked herself up and ran to her car, leaving the battlefield as fast as she could.

Rebecca located a Park Ranger to report the incident, showing her bruises, but the skeptical Ranger shrugged it off, telling her she must have slipped and she had an over-active imagination. What do you think actually happened? Did she indeed have an *over-active imagination* — or was she accosted by an angry specter still fighting the battle near Plum Run?

11

UNLUCKY PENNY

Gettysburg has, over the years, had many occasions with superstition playing a major role in the irrational, or perhaps unexplainable, beliefs associated with the battlefield. One such conviction had its origins beginning decades ago.

Tony, when a young boy, would gather up his neighborhood friends and all would hike across the battlefield, ultimately ending at Devil's Den. Tony and his companions all lived in the area, having the opportunity to regularly play on the battlefield. One day Tony came across something, nothing spectacular or out of the ordinary mind you, just an everyday coin - but this small object would forever change his beliefs in mysticism.

It so happened that on that particular day, Tony was atop Devil's Den, on a large boulder. It was about the highest point in the Den, situated above Smith's Battery in front of the 99th Pennsylvania monument. While playing 'Yanks' and 'Rebs', Tony selected that boulder for its advantageous height, allowing him an excellent view of the area. It was then, as he stood on the boulder, that he glanced down at his feet and something caught his eye. Laying in a depression on the boulder, partially covered by a small stone, he found a coin — a Lincoln-head penny. No sooner did he spot the penny, when his friend Peter joined him atop the boulder. Tony showed him his new discovery and Peter began discussing the possible different types of candy they could purchase with the find. As Peter moved the tiny stone and picked up the penny, he jokingly told Tony, "Look, Lincoln is facing in the direction he gave his Gettysburg Address."

Happy with the find, the two boys decided to leave the battlefield and spend the penny, after whetting their appetite with visions of sweet candy. Peter tucked the penny away in his pocket and they started to leave when, after just moments, he lost his footing on one of the rocks, falling onto the hard surface breaking his arm. Fortunately, help was not far away and the poor boy was soon at the doctor's office mending his wound.

After a few weeks, Tony and his friends returned to the

battlefield. This time, their parents who learned of the mishap, sternly warned the boys to be careful on the rocks. Tony's favorite spot was atop the boulder at Devil's Den, so he made his way to it and continued to play. To his complete surprise, he found another penny in the same depression, covered by a small stone — Lincoln facing the same direction! Thinking his pals were playing a joke on him, he called them over and pointed out the penny asking who placed it there. The boys were bewildered and none

The 99th PA monument with "Penny Rock" to the left

claimed to have put it there. Besides, these particular children did not have money to be throwing around, especially considering a penny could buy something in those times. Still not believing his friends, Tony said, "Oh well, guess I got me a penny then." With that he picked up the coin and the boys continued with their play. Then something unexpectedly happened that made young Tony think perhaps his friends did not put the penny there. As they were playing, Tony was pretending he was a general, charging at a full speed run. Usually sure-footed, he tripped, falling face-first onto one of the flat rocks. His nose began to bleed and his eye swelled shut. Tony in tears and pain made his way home, somehow thinking that penny had something to do with it, after all, Peter previously took the penny and also got hurt.

The boys stayed away from Devil's Den for quite some time. After several months, for the most part forgetting the two injuries suffered

30

by them, they ventured back onto the battlefield and ultimately to Devil's Den. Tony, with Peter and another friend Jim, stepped on top of their favorite boulder. To their astonishment and disbelief, there it was, just like the others, and covered by a small stone — a penny with Lincoln facing the same direction! This time though, Tony and Peter having previous ominous circumstances linked to the penny, refused to pick it up. However, Jim, telling them how silly they were acting, did not hesitate to take the penny, even as Tony pleaded with him not to do it. As they continued with their play, Tony kept insisting Jim return the penny to the spot he found it. Then it happened — Jim, almost identical to Tony's mishap, lost his footing and tumbled down, breaking his index finger. In excruciating pain, Jim beseeched Tony's forgiveness for not believing him, as he now too, became a victim of the mysterious appearing pennies.

Time went on and as the boys grew older, they did on occasion venture back to Devil's Den. At times reporting that they indeed did see the mysterious penny in the same spot, however, refusing ever to take it, for they now knew the consequences. As they aged and reflected back on their most unfortunate experiences, they firmly believed that, while unsure of how the penny was placed there, it was meant to ward off the evil spirits from Devil's Den. Not only was it considered bad luck to remove the penny, but as they could attest to, chances of something bad happening to them were quite high.

We should note that over the years those boys and unrelated parties, have come across a penny on that boulder and, after picking it up, received various degrees of misfortune. We have also heard that from time to time pennies have been left there for good luck. Although we have not come across the penny ourselves, others in very recent years have. We can only say that if we do have the opportunity to see the penny, it will definitely remain where it is. If you see it, do what you may — but remember the dire consequences that could be awaiting you if you choose to take it.

12

PICTURE OF DEATH

One summer day several years ago, Bill, a longtime resident of Gettysburg, had some time to himself and ultimately decided to do one of his favorite pastimes — visit the battlefield. One of his hobbies was photography, so he seldom left his home without his camera, never knowing when or where that 'perfect shot' would present itself. Bill placed his camera and equipment in his car and soon was on his way.

Although the day was pleasant as far as the temperature, it was lightly raining, not enough though, to discourage Bill's venture to the battlefield. No sooner did he drive through the main entrance off Emmitsburg Road, than the rain stopped, the sky cleared and a beautiful day presented itself. Bill took full advantage of the weather, using the sun-filled sky shining upon the wet ground and glistening off objects, to create splendid views for his photographs. Special to him were the picturesque rock formations created by the many boulders found throughout the battlefield in their stoic grandeur. As he made his way to Little Round Top, Bill slowly walked along, reading the plaques on the monuments just as he had done often before. While he was trying to imagine the grotesquely bloody slaughter that took place on the battlefield, he occasionally took a photograph of an interesting statue or scene.

It was already midday and many tourists were around and about the area. Bill, a pleasant fellow, loved to carry on conversations with the other visitors and gladly answered their questions regarding the battle, often volunteering fascinating accounts of the fighting. He even found some tourists so engrossing, like Tom and Mary, that he exchanged addresses with them hoping for future letters.

Explaining to the small group of tourists what had taken place between Little Round Top and the surrounding area, Bill went with them down the hill, through the Valley of Death to Devil's Den. He explained the terrible battle and the resulting bloodshed on both sides. Showing them the crevices and natural fortification of the huge boulders, he pointed out where several Confederate soldiers were killed. As Bill was telling them about the gruesome deaths, he noticed another person joined the group. He was a soldier, wearing a floppy hat dressed in gray, possessing an odor of sulfurous gunpowder. Believing the person was a Civil War reenactor, Bill was impressed by the authentic-looking gray uniform, complete with dirt, worn-out knees and shredded trouser bottoms. Not only did his uniform look genuine, but the Confederate Soldier did not appear to have a tooth in his head, nor was he wearing any shoes. Of course Bill thought that was a little too much, after all, with sharp rocks and snakes found around Devil's Den, the bare foot would be no match against them.

Bill, the tourists, and his new-found friends Tom and Mary, were so impressed with the Confederate soldier, they asked if they might take his picture. The shabby soldier silently gazed at them, then nodded his approval, the group hurriedly grabbed their cameras and began taking pictures, even, at times, posing with him.

Finished with the picture taking, Bill and the group resumed talking. Wondering where the man was from and what reenacting group he was with, they turned looking for him, but he was nowhere in sight. Quite astonished by the soldier's quick exit, Bill thought they were just so engrossed in conversation, they never noticed him leave.

Bill visited a few more sites on the battlefield before leaving, but he could not help visualizing the ragged Confederate soldier. The whole time he got a bizarre feeling associated with the man. Bill could not wait to get his film developed and see the photograph of the soldier, hoping that it might be one of his best yet to add to his fine collection.

After several days, he picked up his developed film and, too anxious to wait until he got home, immediately opened the envelope to examine the pictures. There he saw exquisite photographs of monuments, beautiful scenery, and then the ones he was waiting for, the soldier at Devil's Den. Nevertheless, Bill was in total shock when he looked at the pictures — the boulders and tourists posing at Devil's Den were there — but none, not one, showed the elusive Confederate soldier! "How could this be?" he thought, "I took at least five pictures of him, some of him alone, others of tourists posing with him." Bill could not believe what happened and quickly wrote letters to Tom and Mary, the tourists he met that day, asking how their photographs turned out. The answered letters came back, and Tom wrote him that they must have ruined the film because none came out. Mary's pictures were ironically the same as Bill's

— Mary, who posed with the Confederate, was now standing alone.

We should note here that many others have had a variety of problems associated with picture-taking at Devil's Den. For one possible explanation to that phenomenon, we must look back to July of 1863. Most people are familiar with the famous Timothy H. O'Sullivan photograph of the dead sharpshooter. The soldier is laying behind the rock entrenchment at Devil's Den. What is not commonly known, however, is that O'Sullivan dragged the lifeless body of the young man

Devil's Den — many people have experienced problems with cameras and film here

from the field some yards away, to the rocks — for the sole purpose of staging a dramatic photograph. It has been said that the spirit of that Confederate soldier, angry over being moved from his original resting place, still prowls the Den causing cameras and film to malfunction for retribution.

There is no doubt in Bill's mind that what he and the group of tourists witnessed that day at Devil's Den, was a spirit from the Battle of Gettysburg, for whatever reason, still walking the battlefield. If per chance you wish to visit Devil's Den and happen to encounter a lone Confederate soldier, examine him closely — for he may be the phantom sentry.

13

IF LOOKS COULD KILL

Both during and after the filming of *Gettysburg*, scores of Civil War reenactors were drawn to the mystique of the battlefield. Of these, there have been many with frequent reports of unusual occurrences, ranging from strange sounds and smells, to actually seeing illogical visions. One explanation is, because reenactors customarily dress in uniforms while visiting the battlefield, the spirits see them as familiar or "one of the boys." These sightings or visualizations happen more than have been reported. Many remain untold simply because the person or persons involved do not think people will believe them, or possibly they feel what they saw was just their imagination. Yet of the many reports, the main subject seems to be soldiers, Confederate and Union, randomly appearing day or night on all parts of the battlefield. This is not unusual when one considers the immensity of the battle. On July 1, 2 and 3, 1863, more men died at Gettysburg than any other battle on this continent — upwards of 50,000 dead and wounded. With so many souls suffering horrifying deaths, is it any wonder so many people make contact with apparitions?

One of the many reports occurred several years ago during July to a group of Confederate reenactors portraying a Virginia infantry unit. The group consisted of five men, gathered with thousands of others for a once-in-a-lifetime event, the 130th anniversary reenactment of the Battle of Gettysburg. The Virginia group set up camp along with the other reenactors, partaking in a variety of 'living history' events, sightseeing, and just plain having fun.

The third day there, they had a very long day, filling every minute with as much excitement as possible. They knew soon they would have to leave Gettysburg, perhaps never again to return. As the evening approached, the Virginia group, still dressed in their Confederate uniforms, left their campsite to once again tour the battlefield, soon arriving at Devil's Den. They had all been there several times and suggested walking up to Little Round Top, to which they quickly agreed, 'hoofing' up the paths.

Once up the hill they decided they should not miss the area of the 20th Maine charge before parting, and shortly were walking through the woods. As they walked, examining everything in sight, they commented on the bizarre feeling they were getting in the densely wooded section of the hill. It was twilight with patches of fog in the vicinity, when one man thought he saw someone ahead. Sure enough, out of the fog emerged three Confederate soldiers with forbidding looks on their faces, dressed in ragged and torn uniforms. The Virginia reenactors all stopped and watched curiously as the three Confederates approached, none speaking, just examining the reenactors. When the three were close enough, the Virginia men, thinking they were also reenactors, asked with what group they were. No response. They thought they did not hear and again asked the same question, but again, no response. The three mysterious men, now only several feet from the group, stopped momentarily to observe the reenactors, then walked off.

Quite bewildered, the Virginia group watched as the three Confederates walked into the fog, even more astonished when the soldiers vanished. A few of the reenactors quickly ran to the spot they last saw the three men, but not a trace of any of them was to be found. The Virginia reenactors, dumbfounded, looked at each other for confirmation on what they had just witnessed. They concluded that they were visited by three phantom Civil War soldiers. The reenactors believe that, after being scrutinized, the apparitions were satisfied they were no threat to the Confederacy, and continued on their timeless vigilant journey, back into their clandestine world.

-14-

STORMY WEATHER

Tim and Michael, avid reenactors, both love the outdoors and in particular, camping. For them, the two activities, reenacting and camping, were ideal and they could not find better ways to spend their spare time.

They learned of a reenactment that was held in Gettysburg, the Mecca to many Civil War reenactors. The two had been to Gettysburg before and enjoyed every minute of it, which prompted their decision again to make the trip.

They packed all their gear and soon arrived in the peaceful town. As usual, they toured the battlefield, just as enchanting as always. The day was beautiful and pleasant, without rain in the forecast, which delighted them. As they toured, Tim and Michael discussed where they would camp for the night, suggesting many places. Toward late afternoon, they decided upon an isolated site they hoped would be relaxing. The spot they chose for their tent was in the confines of Pitzer Woods.

As the men put up their tents and set the stakes in the ground, Tim looked around and commented how fortunate they were to have such a pleasant day. Not only were they reenacting the next day, they were camping in Gettysburg on the actual battlefield, on a splendid day.

Pitzer Woods

They took in as many sights as daylight would allow them, and when darkness took over, sat in their candle-lit tent. They talked about

39

many subjects that evening, each almost exclusively associated with the battle. Tim and Michael were lamenting on the terrible devastation and casualties of the past battle. They wondered what was going through the minds of the thousands of Lee's retreating Confederates after losing the battle. Michael imagined the seventeen-mile-long line of physically and psychologically exhausted soldiers, devastated by their defeat in Gettysburg. Slowly, those unfortunate soldiers trudged their way back to the safety of their beloved South, every step impeded by a driving rainstorm pounding them unmercifully.

For some unknown reason, Tim and Michael discussed Lee's retreat to quite an extent, even more than any other part of the battle. In fact, at one point Tim commented to Michael, "Why are we talking so much about Lee's retreat? It seems like we've been discussing that for hours." Michael agreed, yet the two involuntarily continued to talk in length about the retreat, well into the late hours of the night. Finally, both men exhausted, bid each other good night and went into their individual tents to sleep.

Tim fell asleep, but woke by the sound of rain hitting the tent. He thought that very strange since the skies were clear during the day and no rain was in the forecast for several days. He dozed off and soon again awakened by a violent rain storm beating against the tent walls. He kept looking for leaks and thought the tent might even blow over from the force of the storm. The man tried to sleep but with the pounding rain, he kept thinking about the terrible mess he would find in the morning. After what seemed like hours, Tim eventually was able to sleep.

The next morning, Tim woke up, and immediately looked around inside his tent for signs of water. He thought to himself, "Ah, Great! I made it through the storm and the tent held together." He was tired and groggy, still, he wanted to leave the comfort of his dry tent to look at the results of the storm. Tim slowly got up and exited his tent. What he saw bewildered him — everything in sight was in place and dry as a bone. He did not see any sign of water, in fact, the ground was powdery-dry. He could not believe it, with a rain like the one he heard the night before, everything should have been flooded and drenched.

Quickly he went to Michael's tent, calling him out. As Michael looked around, he too was dumbfounded with the scene. Both men heard the storm at night and expected the worse in the morning, only to find a beautiful serene spectacle.

Tim and Michael never did find out what happened that night. They asked other people about the storm and all they received was a look of puzzlement, the answer always the same — "What storm?". The two men concluded they encountered some type of paranormal experience. First, with the unexplainable abnormally long discussion of Lee's retreat, then the horrendous rainstorm that only they heard.

As Tim and Michael later found out, all of their experiences took place in the area where many Confederates left for their long march home, on that rainy night so long ago.

-15-

BE CAREFUL WHAT YOU ASK FOR

One July a couple of years ago, Robert and Diane arrived in Gettysburg for a one-week vacation, far away from their Midwest home. Although Robert had been there several times before, it was Diane's first visit to the well-known battlefield. The couple met some friends who were residents and, together, they traveled the grounds pointing out many sites. After a couple days of sightseeing, Robert suggested to Diane to see the battlefield at night. He jokingly warned her of the spirits that haunt the battlefield, particularly at night. They made the decision and they were on their way to a nighttime tour of the place.

Spot at Devil's Den where Diane taunted the spirits

The serenity of the area intrigued Diane in the dark, but hardly the least bit worried about 'ghosts'. One favorite place on the battlefield, according to Robert, was undoubtedly mystical Devil's Den. Here was an area filled with tales of haunting, just the right place for Diane to experience the unknown. It was quite dark as they drove into the parking

43

lot next to the large boulders of Devil's Den, perfect for uninvited guests.

Robert and Diane made their way to the top of the boulders, with the aid of a small flashlight. They turned off the light and, in the calm of the evening, talked about the horrors of the battle, including the deaths occurring at Devil's Den. After about fifteen minutes, Robert started talking about the supposed ghosts in the area. Diane listened intently, but mockingly challenged any ghost to dare show up. As expected, not a single ghost was seen. Not even so much as an unusual sound was heard that evening.

As they left, Diane told Robert, "I told you so," as she laughed. Robert, however, did not rule out any abnormal sightings and, although he joked earlier, he did believe 'strange' things happened at Gettysburg.

For the rest of their vacation, the couple enjoyed a variety of activities. Soon, however, they found they had just one day left before they had to leave. Cramming as much as possible into their last day, the two returned again to Devil's Den late in the evening — for one last look. Already dark, they made their way atop the boulders to say farewell and goodbye. Diane spoke out, telling the ghosts she was leaving, and sarcastically invited them to get into the car and come along. Both found the statement amusing and the next day were on their way home, back to the Midwestern prairies.

One evening about a month later, Diane was alone in her family room reading a magazine, when movement caught the corner of her eye. Startled, she quickly looked up. For an instant she thought she saw the shape of a man, but nothing was there. She was not really concerned until a week later, again in the evening and again alone. This time as she watched TV, Diane swore she saw a man in the adjacent room. She sprang up from the chair, only to find the room was empty.

Now Diane was worried because twice she thought she saw a man in the house. She contemplated telling Robert of the visions, but stopped short for fear of ridicule. Another month went by and Diane completely forgot the two incidents until late one evening. Engrossed in a book, Diane sat by herself, with the television on and volume low. Suddenly, she had a strange feeling she was not alone and lifted her head, looking into the other room. There it was again! She swore that same man's images momentarily appeared, just long enough to get a quick glimpse, and then was gone. "What on earth is going on?", Diane thought to herself. "Am I losing my mind?" In her quick sighting, she saw the man wearing a loose-fitting shirt, trousers with suspenders, and a floppy hat upon his head. Still unsure whether or not to tell Robert, she thought it over, and decided to withhold her visions.

From time-to-time, Diane would see, or thought she saw, the lonely image of the man. Ironically, while Diane was having her phantom visitations, Robert was going through much the same thing. He too, was reading a book in the quiet hours of the evening, when much to his surprise he believed he saw a person in the next room. This happened to him not once, but several times. Just as had happened to Diane, the image would only stay an instant, then quickly vanish. Robert at first was going to tell Diane, but changed his mind. He remembered telling her of the ghost stories in Gettysburg and watching her laugh them away. He did not want to be humiliated by telling her more stories of the supernatural. After all, she did not believe before, why would she now?

As with Diane, Robert witnessed the visions many times over the next months. They were always the same, just appearing for an instant. Each time they wondered if they really saw a man, or were their minds playing tricks on them. Both kept their secret from the other.

Close to a year after touring the battlefield, the couple's friend from Gettysburg drove to the Midwest to visit with them. They engaged in casual conversation and later found themselves talking about their last time in Gettysburg. Diane finally felt at ease enough to speak of the sightings in her house and went on to tell her friend John what she thought she saw. Hearing this, Robert was speechless. He could not believe it. The same thing happened to him and both described the man exactly! Robert then told his experiences and the two could finally relieve their minds of the secret burden. They were absolutely in awe. They thought about what happened over the past year and both were convinced that, when Diane 'invited' the ghosts to come back with them, that is exactly what happened! Although not physically bothered by the visions of the man, Robert and Diane thought the ghost belonged in Gettysburg. Diane said it worked before, and with that, sternly told the ghost to get into the car and go back with John.

With that, neither Robert nor Diane were ever visited again by the image of the man. However, the story does not end here. John returned to Gettysburg and after a few days, noticed strange things begin to happen. He thought it peculiar that he was frequently misplacing items in his home. He would remember exactly where he left something, but when he went to get the object, it was moved or gone. One night he wanted to light a cigarette, and finding his lighter empty, used matches instead. John placed the empty lighter on his bed and the matches on the dresser, then walked out of the room. Minutes later, he reentered the room and to his surprise, neither the matches nor the lighter was there! He thoroughly searched the whole room, and when done, the other room — without success. Frustrated, he walked to a nearby store to purchase a new lighter. Upon his return, he was shocked as he opened the door — there were the lighter and matches!

Occasionally, John came back to the room in disarray, with clothes strewn about, drawers emptied, and papers scattered around. It is John's belief that the same ghost that frequented Robert and Diane's home did indeed return with him to Gettysburg — and now resides in his home. Only this time, the apparition is showing disapproval over the new residence. The dissatisfaction may be because the apartment, they say, is built upon the graves of Civil War casualties.

16

INTO THE NIGHT

They created Memorial Day for one reason — remembrance of war dead. However, for one man, it will always mean more.

The year was 1987. Harry and his friends, Tom and Stan, were graciously invited to visit the owner of an old farmhouse. The quaint building, located about three miles outside Gettysburg, was built on the grounds of the gallant cavalry clash between two of the Civil War's most noted heros.

East Cavalry Field

East Cavalry Field is the name given to the ground where dashing Confederate General J.E.B Stuart met head-on with the fearless General George Armstrong Custer. They made history that July afternoon of 1863, as the young union general held off Stuart, preventing certain devastating results to the Union Army, engaged only miles away.

Harry and his companions were thrilled with the prospect of

spending time on an actual battlefield, and such a famous one at that. They had started a bonfire and the men grilled steaks for a meal that would make any chef envious. They finished their food as they sat around the fire reminiscing about the Civil War battle that took place on that very spot. It was already dark and late in the evening, so Harry, Tom and Stan decided to call it a night. Harry went in the farmhouse to brush his teeth and wash up, then bidding the homeowner goodnight, walked back to his car. The three men planned on sleeping there for the night and each went to prepare their 'sleeping quarters'.

Tom and Stan rolled out their sleeping bags near the huge bonfire, knowing it would burn all night. Harry walked over to his station wagon, and because it was a pleasant night, opened the rear tailgate to allow more room. Rolling out his sleeping bag, he carefully removed any obstructions so he could have a very restful night. By this time, it was quite dark and the night so still, Harry could have heard a whisper. Crawling into his sleeping bag, he settled in and began to relax making for a good night's sleep.

Just as his head touched the soft pillow, Harry had a feeling someone was there. As he picked his head up and slowly looked to his left, he saw a man dressed in the uniform of a Union cavalryman. Startled, he quickly scurried out of his sleeping bag, but to his amazement, the man was gone. Questioning what he just saw, Harry surmised his friends, Tom and Stan, were playing a practical joke on him. He walked to the still-large bonfire to tell them what a frightening joke they played on him. Harry stopped in his tracks when, at the bonfire, he saw both Tom and Stan sound asleep! Memorial Day now has a deeper meaning to Harry. He will never forget the war dead — especially the cavalry!

17

A CHILLING TRIO

Gettysburg was the site of a reenactment July 1989, drawing hundreds of Civil War enthusiasts for the event. For Larry, Daniel, and Paul, the event would forever change their beliefs about the supernatural.

Vicinity of Hunt Avenue where three images appeared

It was about 10:00 p.m., and the three men were exhausted from a long day of reenacting. Larry parked his car across from Meade's headquarters, the Union rear during the Battle of Gettysburg, and the men exited the car. Although they were tired, the excitement of the reenactment kept their adrenaline flowing. Thus, they decided to walk down the dark and lonely Hunt Avenue to unwind. They walked only a short distance, when suddenly, three dark figures appeared only fifty feet from them. Not close enough to make out faces, they could identify that each figure was wearing a large-type hat, similar to that of the Civil War.

Not too concerned, Larry said they were most likely other

reenactors from the filming of the movie *Gettysburg*, and they continued. However, as they moved on, the three shadow-figures also moved. Larry, Daniel and Paul kept walking, randomly changing direction to see if the pattern continued. Each time they moved, the dark images followed accordingly, always stopping to their left. It seemed to them they were deliberately being followed and observed.

Now concerned, the three reenactors quickly went into a field to their right. As they looked around, sure enough, the shadows again moved to their left, to an open field. The three men had mixed emotions, fright, fear, and many other thoughts. This time Larry suggested they find out who was following them and why. Reluctantly, they started to approach the three dark figures for a closer look, and as they got nearer, the images disappeared. In front of the three men was nothing but a large empty field. They took out a flashlight and scanned the area as far as they could see. Nothing! Not another person could be found.

Larry and his friends believe, because they were dressed in Confederate uniforms, the three shadows were none other than apparitions of Union soldiers, still protecting their positions.

-18-

JUST BEING NEIGHBORLY

When the filming of the movie *Gettysburg* was taking place, thousands of people were recruited as extras. Many were reenactors, arriving with complete equipment and uniforms, while others were brought in from the town and supplied with uniforms. During the filming, numerous strange and unexplainable occurrences took place. To this day, several of those stories are still haunting the memories of the people touched by them. With such a mass of people on the battlefield dressed in Civil War uniforms, is it any wonder why so many witnessed the unexplainable?

Some people believe that the mere presence of the familiar, as with the uniform-clad reenactors, brings out the spirits. Gregory and Brad, two hard-core reenactors, were part of the filming and, to their displeasure, part of the unexplained.

Many movie extras had an area set aside for use as a camp. Here they set an array of tents — temporary quarters — where many would stay weeks at a time. The two men put their A-frame tent amid the others and soon settled in with their comrades, in 'a tent city'. The days would be long and tiring with frequent physical activity such as marching, drilling, and running. To make matters worse, they carried full gear, weighing them down. The hot day would at times take its toll on unsuspecting extras, prematurely sending them home. Nevertheless, Gregory and Brad would not let the long days or the heat prevent them from participating in the once-in-a-lifetime event. They would rarely finish a day of filming without returning to their camp completely exhausted. However, for the two men, they began experiencing strange occurrences, usually late in the evening.

Several times on different nights, they heard voices while they sat by their campfire. The voices sounded near and directed toward them, yet every time they looked around, no one was in the vicinity. The other tents were too far for anybody's voice to travel that far and that clear. It was always the same, as Gregory and Brad sat talking to each other, unknown voices would interrupt them, still, nobody was there.

51

After the usual early starting time and a full day of filming, they finally were released for the day. It was a warm, foggy August night and many movie extras had gone home to reenter, as they would say — the 'real' world. As for Gregory and Brad, they went back to their A-frame tent and plopped down for a well-deserved rest. Because of the series of voices they heard on previous nights, the men looked around for any signs of people nearby. As before, nobody was close. They started a campfire, just as every night before, and discussed what had happened during the day. In the back of their mind, each of them could not forget the unexplained voices.

Late in the evening, the two men decided it was probably time to retire for the night. With that, they went into their tent. The exhausted Brad, although frightened from the many voices they heard over the weeks, fell asleep almost instantaneously. Gregory, on the other hand, could not sleep that night.

It was 3:00 a.m. and Gregory sat in the tent thinking about the Gettysburg battlefield. He thought, too, of the movie he was part of and wondered how it would turn out. He went out of his tent to check on the campfire, when, to his complete surprise, he saw an officer's tent. The tent had to be there for a couple hours, for it had a perfect campfire burning in front of it. Gregory was amazed because the new tent was only a few yards away. He could not understand how someone could possibly pull up a car, set up the tent, drive the stakes in, and build a fire, without making a sound.

Still baffled, Gregory thought it must be fatigue and with that, reentered his tent. He was sure they were more reenactors and would greet them early in the morning. Soon Gregory was sound asleep.

In the morning, the two men arose and began dressing in their uniforms. As he was dressing, Gregory asked Brad if he heard the new people drive in last night and set up their tent. He looked puzzled and told Gregory he did not hear a thing during the night. They finished readying themselves for the movie and left their tent to introduce themselves to the new neighbors. They stood there in disbelief as they looked around — neither a tent nor a fire pit was to be found! Not one sign of any human being in that spot, no car tracks, no grass trampled down, nothing! Gregory and Brad could take no more. They finished that day of filming *Gettysburg* and packed their gear, having had enough of the spirit world.

19

AN UNEXPLAINED FIRE

Another story told during the filming of the movie *Gettysburg* involves yet another tent. In August of that year, the set was packed with movie extras. For most, the main reason they traveled to Gettysburg was to be a part of the historically significant movie and to experience the feel of a real battlefield. For three of the thousands of extras, an experience of a different sort took place.

The reenactors' camp was set up with a Union and a Confederate side. Three men, Edward, Ted and Hank, were part of the Union forces and camped accordingly.

One morning, about 3:00 a.m., only a handful of men were awake. The small group, which included the trio of friends, was in the Union side of the camp. One reenactor sat strumming softly on his guitar. Edward and his friends were having an enjoyable time telling stories and talking about the filming that took place during the day. Even with the long day each had to endure, the men slept little, living to the fullest the 'experience' of Gettysburg.

Behind their tent was a row of canvas A-frame tents, nothing special, the same as the men had seen hundreds of times before during their reenactments. The men talked for about fifteen minutes and for some strange reason, had the urge to turn around and look at the row of tents to their rear. Before they had a chance to say anything, a most unusual thing happened. Seconds later, as they stared at the row of A-frames, the tent directly behind theirs lit up and burst into flames. The three of them, as quick as their feet would take them, rushed to the flaming tent. Fearful that people may be in the tent, Edward smashed through the burning tent in an attempt to pull them to safety. Fortunately, all that was in the tent were blankets and gear. Apparently, the extras had gone into the town for the night. This turned out to be a move that could have saved them serious injury or worse. The fire was too intense to retrieve any of the objects inside it, so the men using better judgment backed away letting nature take its course.

After the fire was out, the only thing that remained was a

smoldering tent and many unanswered questions. The owners of the destroyed A-frame returned early next morning to find no more than a pile of ashes. Ted reported the story and asked if they had left a candle in the tent or perhaps a campfire still lit. The men steadfastly denied leaving their tent in any unsafe condition, as they always double-check before they leave. With no logical explanation to the igniting of the tent, Edward and the others came to one strong possibility. They believe the ghosts of the Confederacy, unhappy with the 'Yankees' camping on the hallowed ground, purposely caused the tent to burn in an effort to say — "Go away!" "You're not welcome!"

20

A PSYCHIC CONNECTION

Some people are gifted with what often is called a 'sixth sense', the intuitive ability to perceive what 'normal' people cannot. One woman, Jan, had the capability of 'tuning in' to supernatural forces with mysterious sensitivity. Fascinated by her own psychic abilities, she seemed to be drawn to 'hot spots' where she would then have mystical experiences. A favorite and natural place to experience her powers, was the hallowed ground of Gettysburg where so many horrifying deaths occurred. Jan had been at Gettysburg often and decided to make the trip yet again. She talked to her husband Jim, and together they set their sights on the old battlefield, hoping for a glimpse of lingering spirits.

In November, the two people arrived in Gettysburg and selected a local motel for the evening. Because they arrived late in the day and were exhausted from the trip, any tour of the battlefield was out of the question until the next day. After a bite to eat, they went back to the motel and planned on a good night's sleep so they could get an early start. Jan sat at the small desk in her room and began to read a book in the hopes of relaxing. It was late and outside was just the stillness of the night, interrupted only by an occasional car passing.

She was getting drowsy and started slowly to close her eyes, when she had a feeling someone was watching her. Her eyes at once opened wide and as she turned around, she saw the distinct likeness of a Confederate soldier standing in the corner of the room. Moments later the vision vanished and Jan was puzzled by what just happened. She wondered whether it was only her imagination or possibly a dream because she was almost sleeping at the time. After that, she thought it best to put the book away, lay in bed and go to sleep.

She could not have been sleeping more than a half hour when she heard what she thought was a faint voice. The light of the florescent motel sign filtering in, dimly lit the room, barely enough, but still sufficient to make out any object in the room. Upon hearing the voice, Jan sat up in her bed, looked around, and saw nothing. She stayed in that position about ten minutes until she became sleepy and laid back down. She looked at her clock and thought to herself she better get some sleep if she wanted to wake early.

This time she found it more difficult to sleep, yet, after about fifteen minutes was fast asleep. Again Jan was awakened from a deep sleep with the sound of a mysterious voice, and again she sprang up to look around. Only this time, as she turned her head, she saw the spirit of the same Confederate soldier she witnessed earlier. She knew she could not be dreaming and looked upon him with both curiosity and fright. Jan could see the man's face intensely staring at her and immediately felt she was unwelcome. Sitting in her bed, she could not take her eyes off the phantom figure, as if she were spellbound. After what seemed like minutes of eye-contact, the Confederate soldier in a haunting voice said, "Go home," and with those words slowly disappeared. For the rest of the night, Jan tried to sleep, waking frequently with the thought of the mysterious visitor.

She woke early the next morning, troubled by her visitor, and quickly told Jim all that she had seen and heard. As she told him what happened, he was so intrigued by the story he began to get chills from the very thought of a spirit. With what he had just heard, Jim was anxious and could not wait to visit the battlefield in search of the unfamiliar. It was Remembrance Day, and a pleasant day as the two of them drove to the battlefield. Although they had their jackets, it was a sunny day without a trace of a cloud in the sky, making it comfortably warm. Jim suggested a few 'hot spots' on the battlefield to walk, like the Wheatfield, Little Round Top, and Culp's Hill. They traversed those areas and nothing out of the ordinary occurred, although from time-to-time Jan would get an unexplained 'feeling'. Jim was disappointed, expecting they would surely encounter a spirit, or if lucky, hear some mysterious voices.

The previous night's visitation from the Confederate soldier, telling her to go home, still bothered Jan. She had no clue why he appeared and told her to leave. As she was thinking about the experience, Jan had a yearning to go to Devil's Den. There was no argument from Jim, trusting her judgment and still wanting to be part of a spiritual occurrence, they were soon on their way.

They arrived shortly in the area of Devil's Den with its maze of rocks and boulders. A short distance away is the aptly named Valley of Death, where many soldiers died a merciless death. Nearby was the Slaughter Pen, where a great many Confederates were killed, some falling between the rocks into the crevices. On July 2, 1863, Confederate General Hood's Division fought a desperate bloody battle with the loss of many lives, eventually capturing Devil's Den at a high cost. Dead bodies were scattered in every direction, along with the pitiful wounded screaming and begging for help.

Imagining all the horrid carnage of the battle, Jim carried his video camera and with Jan, began to walk the locality in search of an 'unusual feeling'. They commented on what a beautiful day it was with plenty of warmth and sunshine. Jan almost immediately began to get strange sensations. She walked over the small footbridge crossing 'Bloody Run' and started to get heavy feelings of sadness, almost enough to make her weep. She could sense the terrible pain and agony the young men felt as they breathed their last breath of life, more than a hundred and thirty years ago.

Jan continued on the path, and with each step of the way, experienced persistent feelings of melancholy. Jim could only look upon Jan with envy, wishing he too could experience what she was going through. The two walked a little farther on the path when the air suddenly got colder, as if they walked into a refrigerator. Finally Jim's wish came true. Inexplicably, the temperature dropped significantly in an instant, and

Frame from the videotaping done by Jan and Jim

this time he experienced it too! This was to be a bone-chilling experience for him in every sense of the word. He quickly grabbed his video camera with hopes of capturing some strange phenomenon on tape. His anxiety was now heightened, however, Jan wanted to leave. Abruptly, a violent wind rushed in, immediately followed by snow. In the midst of the confusion, Jan and Jim heard a voice saying, "Its time to go home"

57

followed by a painful-sounding groan. Both heard the voices and believed them to be coming from the nearby bridge. As quickly as the wind and snow started, it was gone, and yet, the sun was mysteriously shining. They looked all around them, yet not a soul was in the area. Jim and Jan left the battlefield bewildered and feeling fortunate that the strange occurrence favored them. Jim believes that, because Jan had psychic powers, just by being with her he could witness the unnatural developments. Since then, Jan has continued to have occasional psychic intervals. Yet, as Jim and Jan play the video tape made that Remembrance Day, they still get chills as they watch it and listen to the groan, forever reminding them of the terrible slaughter that took place, many years ago.

They have played the tape many times, but what puzzles them is, all the sounds that were recorded have not diminished in the least — all, that is, except the groan. The groan keeps fading every time they play the tape. It should also be noted here that the video was made in 'reverse imaging'.

'Positive' image of photo with closeup showing mysterious figures

Everything had the appearance of negative images. For the purposes of this story, the image was made into a 'positive'. It became apparent that figures and a horse seemed to be in the upper-right hand side of the frame. When brought to the attention of Jim and Jan, they were totally unaware of anything or anybody while videotaping. What, then, appeared on videotape?

21

EVIL IN THE TRIANGLE

Until the time they visited the battlefield of Gettysburg, most people never experienced ghosts or the supernatural. Yet, once introduced to those fields of violent deaths, many people experience feelings never before felt. For some, it is extended past the point of 'feelings' and they hear unexplainable sounds, voices, and, the most chilling of all, witness obscure apparitions.

Triangular Field

Who are these people? They come from all walks of life, construction workers, lawyers, doctors, clerks, clergy and truck drivers, just to name a few. Neither age nor gender makes a difference. For many, the story is the same or very similar, reporting their first-time encounters. Probably the most frequently heard statement is, "I got a strange feeling on the battlefield." Most have no idea what the feeling means, still, they believe it has something to do with the supernatural forces surrounding Gettysburg

Some people, on visiting the battlefield, have a strong feeling of *déjà vu*, the sensations of being in that spot before, though it is their first time there. A good example would be General Patton, of World War II fame, known to have said on several occasions, "I've been here before," as he walked ancient battlefields. For some people it goes even beyond the *déjà vu* stage, having powerful feelings of being killed in the Battle of Gettysburg.

Still others find they are troubled in certain spots on the battlefield, some so much they are physically unable to go near specific areas. With thousands of people visiting Gettysburg each year, many never experience anything out of the ordinary or have any desire to return. On the other hand, many are moved by their experience in Gettysburg and unexplainably keep returning to the hallowed ground. When asked why they return, one answer often heard is, "I don't know why, I can't explain it, there's just something about Gettysburg that makes me want to come back." Some say because of the thousands of soldiers dying so traumatically and quickly, their spirits remain where they died, unable to make the transition to 'the other side'. For these souls, they are still fighting the Battle of Gettysburg — a haunting reminder of another world.

Although it is impossible to know the exact number of people's encounters with the unexplainable in Gettysburg, particular sections or areas have high frequencies of occurrences. When one studies the reports, it becomes evident that those areas were witnesses to heavy destruction with a tremendous amount of loss of life. One of those places is the Triangular Field. On July 2, 1863, around 4 p.m., Robertson's Brigade of Longstreet's Corps arrived on the field, advancing against Union positions. Later, the 4th and 5th Texas assisted, attacking Little Round Top until dark. Following is just a sampling of the many experiences people have had while at the area of the battlefield known as the Triangular Field.

****

A Confused Air

Recently, Bill and Joan made one of their treks to Gettysburg, anticipating another enjoyable visit. The day happened to be pleasant, partly cloudy and mild. They spent some time in town, going through many establishments browsing and purchasing an occasional item. After that, they decided to take a leisurely tour of the battlefield, with no particular target in mind, just drive aimlessly around.

They slowly drove along the peaceful roads, often stopping to walk out to a monument or marker. Bill remarked that although he has been on the battlefield often, he constantly sees more monuments previously unknown to him. They are simply amazed at the vast number and variety of monuments found on the Gettysburg battlefield. Bill and Joan stopped at some popular spots, Devil's Den, Little Round Top, and the High Water Mark. As expected, they were enjoying a relaxing and pleasurable tour, as they randomly moved across the battlefield. Until this time, neither Bill nor Joan had ever had any unusual experience of any kind associated with the spiritual world. This would soon change.

While walking part of the High Water Mark, Bill suggested they go to the Triangular Field. He did not know why, he just knew he wanted to go there. They finished walking the High Water Mark, entered their car and continued the leisurely journey parking near the Triangular Field. As they walked into the field, Bill remembered what he had read about the struggle that took place there. Walking farther, they remembered the pain and suffering that went on during that terrible time, and soon began to get strange feelings. Both told each other about the peculiar feeling they were experiencing. If only one had experienced it, it would not have been too serious, however, with both affected the same way, they knew something out of the ordinary was taking place.

Reluctantly, they continued, drawn forward by some unknown force. Bill happened to have with him a police scanner, on, but with the volume turned down. Oblivious to the scanner, Joan and Bill were more tuned-in to the strange feelings coming over them, than the muffled sounds emitted by the electronic device. They took a few more steps when the sounds of the scanner got their attention. For some unknown reason, the volume increased dramatically, then as quickly, returned to its previous setting. Temporarily forgetting the Triangular Field, Bill's attention was directed to the malfunctioning scanner, checking the battery connections or any other obvious potential problem. Everything checked out okay and no sooner did he lift his head away, than the scanner again blurted loud sounds. He listened intently and to his surprise, heard channels coming in that were not designed for the scanner, not one, but many! They could not believe what they were hearing. The scanner acting erratic and weird was as if it had been possessed, with no control whatever over the inner workings.

Bill and Joan looked at the scanner, then each other, and without so much as a word, turned about-face and left the field. Once back to their car, Bill tried the scanner — it worked perfectly! They had no doubt in their mind that they crossed paths with a powerful force from another dimension.

****

Ouch

For another person, the Triangular Field would provide a memory in her mind she would never forget. Most encounters with the ghosts are of a nonphysical nature, usually just hearing or perhaps even seeing a phantom. However, occasionally people have been known to be touched by a ghost. Such was the case of a young woman, Kelly, as she ventured onto the battlefield. It was not the first time she was on the battlefield, but for Kelly, it was the first time she ever encountered any abnormal experience.

It was just another typical day at Gettysburg and a group of people, including Kelly, chose to walk the battlefield — at night. What began as an entertaining-filled trip onto the field was to take a bizarre turn for the unsuspecting Kelly. The small group of people walked onto the Triangular Field in the dark of the night, allured by the unknown. As they walked along, they told jokes about the ghosts

Another view of Triangular Field

and sarcastically dared them to show their face. They chuckled and giggled, half-serious about the ghosts appearing, still taunting. Kelly and the others were close enough to hear and see each other, but not close enough to touch.

Walking deeper into the Triangular Field, Kelly could see the others several yards away. She was listening to one of her group tell stories about the dead found on the field, when suddenly and without warning, someone grabbed her by the hair, jerking her head back. She let out a frightful scream, quickly turning to see the culprit, however, much to her surprise, no one was there. Her head ached after the pull, bringing tears to her eyes. The others ran over to her and none saw anything in the area. For Kelly, the Triangular Field will forever hold a haunting memory and reminder that there are powerful and unexplainable forces lingering on that bloodstained ground.

****

The Unexplained

There is a report of one man who started as a skeptic, then reconsidered after several experiences on the Triangular Field. We will call him Jerry. He traveled to the battlefield and specifically to the Triangular Field. Knowing others have reported strange things occurring in that area of the battlefield, he had his doubts and thought it all was a hoax.

On one late afternoon, after sundown, Jerry had a desire to walk the battlefield, and what better place than the Triangular Field. He entered the field by himself and looked around, satisfied that he was alone. Keeping in mind the stories about ghosts, Jerry still believed them to be a joke and walked slowly into the field. He had gone no more than about thirty feet, when in the quiet of the night, he heard footsteps behind him. He knew nobody was there moments before, and he turned around, swore he could see six mystical images of people — where he just walked. As he moved closer, they were no longer visible.

The next time Jerry ventured onto the Triangular Field, his wife and friend accompanied him for the experience. Jerry's mind was fresh with the memory of the phantom visions of his previous trip on the field. The three slowly walked across the field, ever vigilant for abnormal occurrences, and soon found it was time to turn around. They began crossing back over the same field, when after only moments, his friend stopped them, asking where did those men come from. As Jerry, his wife and friend turned and looked back to the spot they had just left moments before, they were all stunned — there again stood the six figures! Jerry has since walked that same field several times, seeing many unexplainable things.

22

THE BEAT OF A DISTANT DRUMMER

The Battle of Gettysburg on July 3, 1863, became known as The High Water Mark of the Confederacy. At 1:00 in the afternoon, General Lee, in an attempt to crush General Meade's troops, chose to attack dead-center into the Union forces, then on Cemetery Ridge. Trying to break up the Union battle lines, Lee instructed his massed artillery to open fire on the unsuspecting men, sending a barrage of deadly shells into their foes.

High Water Mark

To this, the Union soldiers answered with their own lethal volley in a punishing manner. The exchange of artillery fire continued for some time. However, because of the limited vision caused by the powder-darkened skies, Lee's attempt to soften the Union lines was mostly inconsequential. When the guns ceased, General Lee instructed General Longstreet to begin the mass assault on the Union position.

The famed General George Pickett was directed to send his 15,000 Confederates into the center of the Union line in a desperate attempt to break, and ultimately win, the three-day battle. The men marched a mile across the field, each step of the way being bombarded with shot and shell, and when within range, fired upon by volleys of musketry. With dead and wounded rapidly littering the field, the men desperately fought their way forward. The effort was in vain, for only a few could reach the Union line before being driven back. In about an hour it was all but over, there on that bloodstained field were 10,000 casualties. After Pickett's Charge failed, the battle was over and for Meade, a decisive Union victory.

For many reenactors, walking Pickett's Charge is an honor and done in memory of those who died in that futile attempt more than a hundred and thirty years ago. Each person has his or her own reason, but for Mike and Dan, they wanted to experience what it felt like just to walk that same battlefield. However, they would 'experience' more than just a feeling.

On a cool day, Mike and Dan decided it would be a good time to walk the field, and after an early breakfast, drove to the Virginia monument. The sun had just begun to rise and the battlefield was void of any people, perfect for contemplating on the war-dead as they would walk. As Mike and Dan started their stroll, they tried to imagine what was going through the minds of the thousands of Confederates as they faced sure devastation. As hard as they tried, they could not come close to the frightful sight witnessed by the soldiers under Pickett's command.

Slowly continuing across the field, they stopped about a third of the way when both said it seemed as if an energy was all around them. They looked around and still were the only people on that desolate field. Mike and Dan heard of people experiencing a certain unexplainable 'feeling', yet, until then had never personally had it happen to them. Unsure of what was happening, they continued walking, trying to understand the unknown source of energy. When about halfway across Pickett's Charge, Dan stopped again, turned to Mike and said, "Listen — do you hear that?" Listening intently, he heard nothing — until a few steps later, then he too heard it. They could hear the faint beating of a drum, the same beat heard as troops march. Thinking it strange, they concluded other reenactors must have been somewhere close by, also

66

visiting the battlefield in the early morning hour.

They again looked around and as before, not a soul was within their sight. Not overly concerned, Mike and Dan resumed their walk, only to be stopped again by the sound of drums, this time louder. Now troubled by the unexplainable event, they came up with several possibilities trying to ease their minds. Satisfied that the sounds were coming from a distance and carried to them, they started walking. Just when they thought they had the logical answer, the drumming started again, louder than before. Thinking other reenactors playing the drums were getting closer, they could not understand why they did not see them yet. The drum beats continued to get louder, just as if the drummers were approaching Mike and Dan, still, they could see nobody. By now, the mysterious beating of drums baffled the two men. As they stood as still as statues, they heard the drums increase in volume to such an extent, they believed the sound to be coming from only a few feet away! They did not speak or move as the phantom drum beats continued, apparently moving in the direction of the Union side. Mike and Dan stood there, nervous and trembling, hearing the drum beats pass by, then the sound continually diminished until finally they could no longer hear it.

After the initial shock of the unexplainable event, Mike and Dan are forever convinced that they had witnessed first-hand a supernatural event.

23

PICTURE PERFECT

Although frequent, no one can predict when or where they will have a supernatural phenomenon. For many, however, if they stay in Gettysburg long enough, they can almost be assured of having an

Sachs Mill covered-bridge built in 1852

unexplainable experience. One place people have reported getting 'strange feelings' is the picturesque Sachs Mill covered-bridge, built in 1852, one mile west of the Eisenhower Farm. Many people find their way to this beautiful part of the countryside to view part of this country's wonderful and scenic past of a forgotten era.

Beth, like many others, drove to that part of the scenic valley to enjoy the landscape and simultaneously, photograph the old bridge. She arrived there on a beautiful summer day, perfect in every way, parked her car and began walking toward the bridge. Beth leisurely strolled around the area, pausing from time-to-time to snap a picture of the quaint surroundings. As the young woman walked across the majestic bridge, she wondered how many soldiers crossed it during the terrible Battle of Gettysburg. Beth was acquainted with the history of the battle and could not help but reflect on that troubled time of our nation. She went from a relaxed frame of mind, to one of sorrow, as she stood on that old bridge. Not understanding why her feelings changed so suddenly, Beth continued walking across the bridge toward the east end, now trying to forget the disturbing past. What began as a pleasant sightseeing trip soon turned into one of confusion for the bewildered woman. No matter how hard she tried, Beth could not stop thinking about the gruesome battle.

She finished crossing the covered-bridge walking only a short distance when, for no apparent reason, the warm summer air suddenly changed to an ice-cold place. Accompanied by the cold, Beth felt the 'strange feeling' so many experienced on the battlefield of Gettysburg. Beth knew something out of the ordinary was occurring and forced herself to move from that spot. After a few yards, the temperature returned to the normal warmth she felt previously, and was convinced she was the object of a paranormal event. Beth, who is rarely at a loss for words, could not come up with any description of what just happened to her. Having had enough 'excitement', she immediately left the place, returning to town to find answers.

She asked many people if they ever heard of or experienced the 'ice-cold spot' near the covered-bridge. She found out that she was not alone — others had the same incident in the same place. Beth also learned that a legend exists stemming from the time of the battle. It seems that, near the bridge, an old oak tree once stood and on its limbs, were hung several Confederate soldiers, accused of desertion. They have said that the spirits of those unfortunates still linger in that very spot, marked by the unearthly cold surrounding the place of their execution.

24

STAND BY YOUR MAN

Being in Gettysburg, not getting caught up in the magic of its history is impossible. Hardly a person can honestly say they never heard of the famed Pickett's Charge. That raging battle of such proportions

Bryan House — vicinity where body of a female in a Confederate uniform was discovered after Pickett's Charge

resulted in about ten-thousand casualties. Among those thousands they discovered the body of a young female, much to the amazement of all, clad in a Confederate uniform. Her lifeless body was found near the Bryan House, just North of the High Water Mark. That part of the battlefield and aftermath of Pickett's Charge sets the stage for the next account.

A local resident, Judy, has first-hand knowledge of the incident, probably more than she would like. The first time Judy went on that 'field of destruction', she had no idea she would be experiencing a paranormal event. She, like thousands before her, thought it would be a good idea to walk the area to get a feeling of what it was like during the battle.

As Judy walked, she remembered what she had read about the famous assault, trying to picture the chaos and destruction taking place every step of the way. However, when she approached the vicinity of the Bryan House, something happened that could not quite be explained. A strange feeling came over her, one she never had before and could not understand. As she walked over that spot of the battlefield, it was as if an invisible hand reached out and held her. Judy just stood there, puzzled by the overwhelming feeling taking control of her body. It was then that she knew a paranormal event was taking place, though she had no idea what or why. She purposely left that spot and when she did, her conviction was confirmed — the feeling vanished

Although initially frightened by her strange feeling, curiosity got the best of her and she walked directly back to the same spot. It happened again! Judy had no logical explanation for her feelings, yet, she knew something was there — and she wanted it to leave. This time she left the area of Pickett's Charge, puzzled and searching for answers.

Judy began asking questions and reading more about Pickett's Charge in hopes of a clue to help solve the mysterious feeling. However, no answer was found to satisfy her curiosity and Judy remained perplexed with her situation. She did believe some type of supernatural occurrence crossed paths with her and in an attempt to find out exactly what, Judy again returned to that precise spot. Now there was no doubt in her mind — something very strange was going on. As she entered the same location, a bizarre feeling overcame her again, however, this time she had the additional sensation of Déjà vu, something before which she had never experienced. More intent than ever, she left the battlefield searching for an explanation.

A few days later, luck would enter her quest, as she read farther about the ill-fated charge. Much to her surprise, Judy learned that a female dressed as a Confederate soldier was found dead on the battlefield. As far as she could figure out, the body was in the exact spot she so dreaded to be at. It is not known exactly why the woman fought with Pickett's men; some say she wanted to be with her man and did what was necessary to accomplish it — even if that meant posing as a man.

After finding out what happened on that spot, Judy has since been there several times, each time getting strong sorrowful feelings along with a perception of Déjà vu. She now believes it was she, killed on that spot, over one-hundred-and-thirty years ago!

When we hear about experiences such as Judy's, we need to keep an open-mind, challenging our understanding of what can be. Remember, what happened to Judy could just as easily happen to you!

25

WE ARE NOT ALONE

On a cloudy day not very long ago, Joseph and Martha, allured by previous visits to the Gettysburg battlefield, again made the trip. As with many others, they could not seem to get enough of the place and were drawn back repeatedly. They looked forward to each visit, learning new and interesting anecdotes each time. However, on that cool and cloudy fall day, Joseph and Martha were about to embark on a journey of a lifetime.

Their day started the same as all the others, excited about the visit. They were enjoying a leisurely day of browsing and getting acquainted with new parts of the battlefield of Gettysburg. Although they have been close to the Wheatfield before, they never walked it nor read the markers. Joseph and Martha paused long enough to read a tablet describing gruesome accounts of the battle on the Wheatfield.

That field, on July 2, 1863, was turned into what they have described as a 'whirlpool of death' in the late afternoon. The battle raged for two-and-a-half hours as the Confederates under General James Longstreet attempted to crush the line held by the Union troops. Each side held the field at different times, six to be exact. As Longstreet's men forced the assault, the Union sent in reinforcements, pushing back the Confederates. Men on both sides took what little shelter they could find in that open field — the 'stony-hill' and stone wall providing defenses for some. Still, with each renewed attack, men fell wounded and killed in the valiant assault. At about 6:30 p.m., the Confederates began to surround the Wheatfield resulting in the Federals falling back. Pools of blood were on the field, along with the wounded, dead and dying. At the end of the day, General Longstreet's Confederates were victorious and held the Wheatfield.

Now that Joseph and Martha had a better understanding of the terrible loss of life that took place in front of them, they continued their walk onto the field with a solemn attitude. With a slight chill in the air and overcast skies, the battlefield had very few visitors that day. As they walked the hallowed-ground of the Wheatfield, they could not help but notice they were alone. "What a difference between today and that ill-fated day of July 1863," Martha remarked. "Back then, this field was packed full of desperate soldiers and today — only the two of us."

They continued their walk to the First New York Light Artillery, Battery D monument. They stood there looking at the impressive monument with its bronze cannon leaning against a spoked-wheel. Martha was talking about the monument when she abruptly stopped in the middle of a sentence and looked at Joseph. Simultaneously, both suddenly had a strange feeling someone was behind them. Quickly turning around, what they did NOT see startled the frightened couple even more — nobody was there. The first words coming out of Joseph's and Martha's mouths were identical — "We are not alone!"

For those that are skeptical, I would suggest taking a walk in the Wheatfield, preferably after dark and alone, and see if you do not get a bone-chilling feeling.

26

THE PEOPLE OF THE LONG HOUSE

Most stories told about the ghosts and spirits of Gettysburg are connected to the Battle of Gettysburg. However, many people reporting strange occurrences assume the apparitions or voices are somehow Civil War soldiers. Remember though, long before Europeans inhabited Gettysburg, the area was home to many tribes of American Indians. History and archaeology prove the existence of tribes local to the area, for thousands of years. It may be that some spirits encountered are not Civil War Era, and could very possibly be that of past Native Americans.

It is well-known that the Triangular Field had many reports of strange occurrences ranging from sounds and voices, to sightings of apparitions. That spot also is very special to one Native American, Little Sunshine, who made a singular discovery while walking on the field. Her story follows, written in her own words, so as not to lose any of the meaning. She narrates the story, first briefly telling who she is, then describes what happened as she made her discovery. Little Sunshine also talks about some of her beliefs and philosophy, to help readers better understand her 'gift from the Creator':

Goei (Hello), I am a Native American and very proud and my people call me Little Sunshine. My bloodlines are very strong, going in four directions. My people are from the Algonquian Nation, of the Mi'kmaq (Micmac) and Narragansetts tribes, also from the Seneca tribe calling themselves Hodinonhsonih — *The People Of The Long House*.

The Creator has been very good to me, he has given me wonderful gifts and I honor all of them. One special gift he has honored me with is the gift to see the spirits of my people. I thank the Creator, My Father, for that gift. The Creator can see in the spirit world and when the Creator honors us with the gift to see the spirits of our people, which is good medicine and we should respect that gift. These gifts are the gifts the Creator will only honor us with if we are on a good road. We are all honored with wonderful gifts, yet human beings just do not know how to use them or do not want to be bothered using them. It is so sad when that happens as time passes by and life gets shorter.

Since I came to Pennsylvania and visited the battlefield a long time ago, many years have passed. Then I had a vision of a sacred village somewhere on the battlefield of Gettysburg, however, I did not know where it could be found. Nevertheless, one day I was walking around the battlefield and there it was — the sacred place I saw in my vision. Years would pass and I met many people that in time would become my friends. My friends asked me one day if I would like to go to the battlefield, saying they would tell me all about the battle and show me around. We went to Devil's Den and up farther to a place they called the Triangular Field — I would call it The Village. It was there that my vision took place, where my spirit world was, and my people — my ancestors — were. *Ah ho*.

Little Sunshine sketched the village as she saw it in her vision

Of course I did not tell anyone in fear they would laugh at me or would not understand, for this place is very sacred to me. As time went by, I later returned to the spiritual world of The Village. I then arrived to that part of our Mother Earth on top of a hill. There I find an open gate with a stone wall on both sides. As I walk to the gate that is when it all happens to me. Inside me I have wonderful feelings of love and caring — all spiritual feelings. Then I smell fire burning and see the spiral smoke

78

rising to Father Sky. My eyes see so much and my heart feels so much, I start to walk through the gate separating this world and my world of spirits. The feelings through my body are so powerful, and the energy flowing around me is so strong, that I can feel my body starting to shake, yet the warmth of my people is felt all around me, and that makes my body become relaxed. With the spirits of my people going through me, now I know that all will be okay. My brother greets me, a tall man with long black hair, wearing leggings and moccasins made of skins from our four-legged ones — a gift that the four-legged gave to us. This is a good

Place where Little Sunshine saw the vision of a sacred village

day, another day of my birth, a day to be with my people. They offer a hand to me, I reach out and take hold of my brother's hand, as he leads me to a path down to the bottom of the village. My eyes see so much — little ones playing, women preparing food, and men sitting in a circle smoking the sacred pipe. The village is so full of happiness, I can see it and smell the smells, I can feel the love the way it was, hundreds of years ago. I am very honored to be here in the village with my people. I am there in the village and our prayer-time and ceremonies begin. As I stand in The Village, the place now called Triangular Field, I want to tell you about the

79

prayer and ceremonies I do while in the spiritual world of my people.

At prayer-time in the village I get my tobacco, put some in my hand, my left hand, for it is closest to my heart. I honor it by holding it up to Father Sky, to the Creator, then turn in the four directions of the circle of life[1]. I then honor the tobacco giving it back to our Mother Earth, as a gift to her. Our Mother Earth has honored all of us with such wonderful gifts; she has given the tobacco for our pipe used for sacred ceremonies.

Mother Earth and Father Sky will give of themselves, so we can eat and keep warm, and for that, we honor them with tobacco and thank them. I thank the winged ones, for they also feed us and honor us with the gift of their feathers, and for the eagle who soars over our Mother Earth, guiding us to safety, as he watches over all of our people. The eagle also brings us words from our Creator. I thank the Rock People, for they have been here a long time before us, and we use the Rock People in our sweat lodges for our prayer-time. I thank the Creator for everything here, on our Mother Earth. The blood of Mother Earth is the most wonderful of all — the water. That is the blood she gives us so we can all survive, for without it, we all would be no more. So I thank her for being so kind, honoring her most wonderful blood and wonderful gifts for us to survive. I use Sweet Grass, which is the hair of Mother Earth, another gift with which she has honored all of us. During our sacred ceremony, Sweet Grass is used for sweetness and harmony. Sage is used for purification; to rid the body of all negative, keeping only positive around us, and to purify our body. We braid Mother Earth's

Little Sunshine honoring the Creator

---

[1] Our people travel in the circle of life and our sacred number is four, for the direction. North is for the Buffalo, it's color is white. East is for the Eagle. it's color is yellow. South is for the Coyote, it's color is red. West is for the Bear, it's color is black. Those are the four sacred colors in the four directions. And thus we honor all the Creator gave us in our circle.

golden hair and I burn the end of a braid. When the smoke appears, I pull the smoke to me, then toward the four directions in our circle of life. I am done with prayer-time in The Village and I look around me. I see the most wonderful smiles on my people's faces, letting me know that all is good and it is another good day for us to be together, here, on Mother Earth. As I walk back to the top of the hill, I stop and turn back to look. My brother tells me I am welcome in the village any time and they will be there to greet me, another day of my birth. When I am at the top of the hill, I look down at the village and see with my eyes, the wonderful people working and the little ones playing. I can hear their laughter and I just smile, then nod my head — I will be back — and my brother smiles. As I walk through the gate, I am in the white man's world once again, remembering I am a Native American, proud, still walking the Red Road with my brothers and sisters by my side.

Seeing Mother Earth and feeling the wonderful energy she gives is hard for the non-Native American. Maybe some day they will be able to use the gifts with which the Creator honored them. Once that happens, they can then use their eyes to see the beauty of our Mother Earth and hear the sounds of happiness and laughter of all the little ones. They will be able to smell the flowers and hear the sounds of the four directional winds. Seeing a leaf fall from a tree (The Standing People), as the leaf falls so gentle upon Mother Earth. They can touch the hair on Mother Earth, to see the blue Father Sky and the white fluffy clouds. There is so little time in our lives. My people will always live the Creator's ways with our love and respect for Mother Earth. Our church is a field and valley, our cathedral the mountains with their ceilings being Father Sky and floor Mother Earth. Our Bible is *Mitakuye Oyasin* (All our Relations), and the pages in our Bible are the trees, the four-legged, the winged-ones, the finned ones, the crawlers, the Rock People, Grandfather Sun, Grandmother Moon, the Star People, and the Thunder. We are all connected, we are all brothers and sisters, we watch all and learn from all. The Creator honored my native people with this Bible. When Grandfather Wind blows, he turns our pages, and they hear the Creator's voice. Our drums we beat, are the heartbeats of Mother Earth — we are the pulses. We believe and respect, we give, and we love. All I have said is from my heart and the Creator and of my people that I can still see and hear as I enter The Village on the Triangular Field. *Ho! Wanishi* (Thank You) - *Ty-ies* (Little Sunshine).

APPENDIX

The maps on the next two pages show the approximate locations where the stories in this book took place. If, for instance, you are interested in the location of story number 14, *Stormy Weather*, look for number 14 on the map. You will see it is near West Confederate Avenue. The second map shows the locations of stories near Devil's Den.

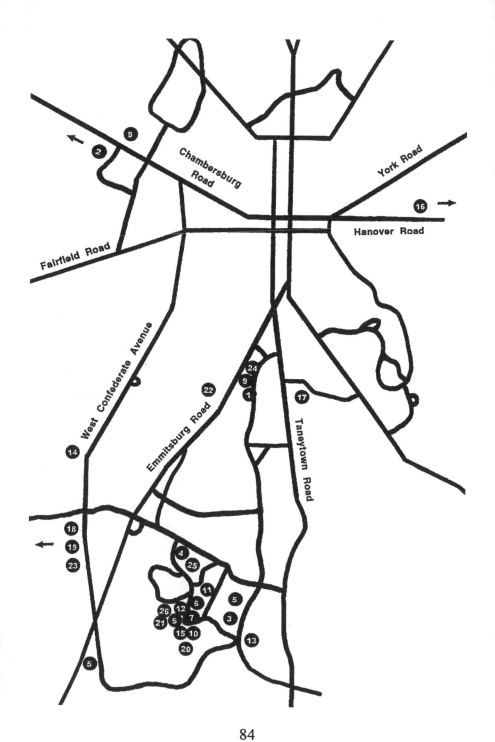

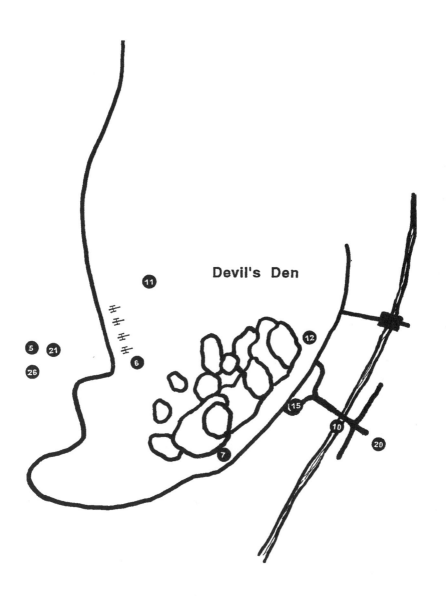

Devil's Den

Have you experienced strange, supernatural, or unexplainable occurrences in Gettysburg? If so, we would like to hear about it for possible inclusion in future publications about Haunted Gettysburg. Please include only first-hand experiences and, if available, photographs you have taken personally. This is your chance to tell your story without fear of ridicule. You are not alone — hundreds, perhaps thousands of people had some sort of unexplained 'ghostly' experience in Gettysburg. If you would like your story told, please fill out and sign the release form and send it to the address indicated for potential inclusion. If your story is used, you will receive a free, personally autographed copy of the book. Your name will not be used unless specifically requested.

- -

Material/Photo Release

TO: Gettysburg R&D
P.O. Box 4561
Gettysburg, PA
17325

I hereby grant to Jack Bochar and Bob Wasel the absolute right and permission to reproduce the material and/or photographs I have supplied to them for inclusion in Haunted Gettysburg and in future reprints and revisions. I further consent to the publication and copyrighting of this book to be published in any manner they may see fit. Proper acknowledgment of my material and/or photos will be made at the author's discretion.

Name _____

Address _____

_____

_____

Date _____

Signature _____

87

your hair's falling out
& your skin is flaky
you walk w/ a limp
~~and~~ & your nose is too big
for your ~~clutless~~ face

your dog ran away &
your woman left you
Amazing that you had a woman at all

you're a loser
yeah yeah
feels bad

you just work you job
at the video store
there's holes in your soul
because your slow